HUMANITARIAN REINSTATEMENT

Attorney Brian D. Lerner

Law Offices of Brian D. Lerner, A Professional Corporation

Attorney Brian D. Lerner

Humanitarian Reinstatement

H-1B Specialty Occupation Visa

Written by Attorney Brian D. Lerner

Print ISBN: 978-1-948774-87-1
Ebook ISBN: 978-1-948774-88-8

INTRODUCTION

There are a multitude of different immigration petitions and applications. They are complex and full of requirements. Obviously it would be best to hire and immigration attorney to best prepare the petitions and application. However, this can certainly cost thousands of dollars.

The next best option is to get a sample of the petition written by an experienced immigration attorney. The samples cost a fraction what would be charged by an immigration attorney. However, while the reader has to alter, amend and change the parts of the sample petition to reflect their actual situation, it is a fantastic roadmap for them to use. If the reader has purchased the entire petition or application, they will have real live samples of cover letters, forms, declarations, affidavits and the necessary exhibits to use. The samples come from real cases and the names of those clients have been redacted to protect the privacy of that person or corporation.

These are petitions and applications that have been drafted by an experienced immigration attorney with over 25 years of experience. Get the benefits of that experience without the costs.

About the Law Offices of Brian D. Lerner

The Law Offices of Brian D. Lerner, APC. The law practice consists of Immigration and Nationality Law and everything involved with and regarding immigration which includes citizenship, investment visas, family and employment visas, removal and deportation hearings, appeals, waivers, adjustment, consulate processing and all types of immigration and citizenship matters. Thousands of families have been reunited and/or permitted to stay in the U.S. and/or return to the U.S. because of the successful work of Immigration Attorney Brian D. Lerner.

This law offices handles all types of immigration cases including family based and employment based. Immigration issues range from immigration court proceedings to trying to fix what paralegals may have done that was neither correct nor proper. Foreign nationals must have experience lawyers admitted to practice law.

The Law Offices of Brian D. Lerner, APC, handles cases arising from business visas, work permits, Green Cards, non-immigrant visas, deportation, citizenship, appeals and all areas of immigration. The Law Offices of Brian D. Lerner, APC does EB-5 Investor Visas, H-1B Specialty Occupation, L-1 Intracompany Transferee, E-2 Treaty Investor, E-1 Treaty Trader, O-1 Extraordinary Ability among others. Regarding immigrant visas for the Green Card, the firm does PERM and advanced degree PERM, Family Petitions, and Extraordinary Alien Petitions. In addition to affirmative petitions, the Law Firm represents people in deportation and removal hearings, including political asylum, withholding of removal, and convention against torture cases.

Brian D. Lerner has been certified as an expert in Immigration & Nationality Law by the California State Bar, Board of Legal Specialization sicne 2000 and has been re-certified three times. He now passes on his decades of experience by allowing the Reader, Law Schools, Professors and other Immigration Attorneys to purchase sample petitions on every facet of Immigration Law.

TABLE OF CONTENTS

About the Humanitarian Reinstatement

Has your immediate relative petitioned you to come to the United States and then passed away suddenly and your I-130 has been denied due to the death of your immediate relative? The best option for you would be the Humanitarian Reinstatement which makes it possible for you to have the I-130 reinstated so you don't have to start the immigration process all over again. Assuming you and the Substitute Sponsor will experience hardship if your I-130 is not reinstated, and the hardship is documented, the Humanitarian Reinstatement will have the best chance for approval. It includes all relevant cover letters, forms, exhibits, and supporting evidence. It has been prepared by an expert Immigration Attorney. Thus, this book will allow you to see a guide of how it's done, prepared and submitted.

SECTION 1
Attorney Cover Letter

Law Offices of Brian D. Lerner
A PROFESSIONAL CORPORATION
CERTIFIED SPECIALIST IN IMMIGRATION AND NATIONALITY LAW
ADMITTED TO THE U.S. SUPREME COURT
LONG BEACH, CALIFORNIA
(562) 495-0554
CARSON, CALIFORNIA
(310) 684-5400

September 26, 2017

U.S. Citizenship and Immigration Services
California Service Center
P.O. Box 30111
Laguna Niguel CA 92607-0111

Re: Humanitarian Reinstatement of Form I-130, Petition for Alien Relative Pursuant to 8 C.F.R. § 205.1(a)(3)(i)(C)(2)
Petitioner:
Beneficiary:
Receipt Number:
Substitute Sponsor/Beneficiary's U.S. Citizen Brother:

Dear Officer:

(hereinafter "Beneficiary") hereby submits the following in support of request that his I-130, Petition for Alien Relative, be reinstated pursuant to 8 C.F.R. § 205.1(a)(3)(i)(C)(2).

TABLE OF FORMS

Forms:	**Description:**
G-28	Notice of Entry of Appearance as Attorney or Accredited Representative of Beneficiary;
G-28	Notice of Entry of Appearance as Attorney or Accredited Representative of Beneficiary's U.S. Citizen Brother;
I-864	I-864, Affidavit of Support Under Section 213A of the INA.

TABLE OF EXHIBITS

Exhibits:	**Description:**
1.	Declaration of Beneficiary;
2.	Declaration of Beneficiary's U.S. Citizen Brother;
3.	Copy of Beneficiary's Certificate of Birth;
4.	Copy of Petitioner's Certificate of Death;
5.	Copy of Approval Notice of Form I-130 of Beneficiary;

6. Copy of Naturalization Certificate of Beneficiary's U.S. Citizen Brother;
7. Copy of Tax Returns of Beneficiary's U.S. Citizen Brother for Years 2013-2016;
8. Copy of Bank Account Statements of Beneficiary's U.S. Citizen Brother; and
9. Copy of Medical Reports of Beneficiary's U.S. Citizen Brother.

I.
STATEMENT OF FACTS

Beneficiary was born on February 19, 1966 in Manila, Philippines. See **Exhibit 3.** Beneficiary has two younger brothers; 46-year-old [redacted], who is a U.S. citizen through Naturalization, and 50-year-old [redacted] who is a citizen of Philippines, and two sisters, 53-year-old [redacted] who is a citizen of Philippines and 48-year-old [redacted], who is a citizen of Philippines.

On December 18, 2008, Beneficiary's U.S. citizen mother, [redacted] (hereinafter "Beneficiary's mother" or "Petitioner") filed an I-130 on Beneficiary's behalf pursuant to INA § 203(a)(2)(B), which was approved on November 19, 2009. See **Exhibit 5.** Unfortunately, Beneficiary's mother died on June 28, 2013. See **Exhibit 4.** Due to Beneficiary's mother's death, the I-130 filed on behalf of Beneficiary has been automatically revoked as of the date of approval pursuant to 8 C.F.R. § 205.1(a).

Beneficiary had already waited for 4 years when Petitioner passed away. Consequently, Beneficiary would have to wait another 23 years for a visa number to become current if his U.S. citizen brother, [redacted] (hereinafter "Beneficiary's brother") were to petition for him at this time. See **Exhibits 1 and 2.**

Beneficiary now prays that his request for Humanitarian Reinstatement be granted pursuant to 8 C.F.R. § 205.1(a)(3)(i)(C), in order that he may be reunited with his brother who is in the United States and eagerly awaiting for his arrival.

II.
BENEFICIARY'S APPLICATION FOR HUMANITARIAN REINSTATEMENT OF THE APPROVAL OF HIS IMMEDIATE FAMILY PETITION SHOULD BE GRANTED IN ORDER TO AVOID HARSH RESULTS CONTRARY TO THE GOAL OF FAMILY REUNIFICATION.

A. Beneficiary Is Statutorily Eligible For Reinstatement Under 8 C.F.R. § 205.1(A)(3)(i)(C) Because Petitioner Passed Away After Approval Of The Immediate Relative Petition.

Pursuant to 8 C.F.R. § 205.1(a)(3)(i)(C), the Attorney General may, in his or her discretion, reinstate the petition for immediate relative upon determination "that for humanitarian reasons revocation would be inappropriate." The Court of Appeals for the Ninth Circuit has further held that, because humanitarian relief under this regulation affords an exception to automatic revocation of "the approval" of immediate relative petition, the exception does not operate unless there has been an approval. *Dodig v. INS*, 9 F.3d 1418, 1420 (9th Cir. 1993).

In present case, Beneficiary's I-130 petition was approved on November 19, 2009. See **Exhibit 5.** More importantly, this approval occurred prior to Petitioner's death on June 28, 2013. See **Exhibit 4.** Consequently, Beneficiary is statutorily eligible for humanitarian reinstatement under 8 C.F.R. § 205.1(a)(3)(i)(C).

B. Humanitarian Reinstatement Is Warranted In The Instant Case As The Alternative Would Necessarily Lead To Harsh Results Contrary To The Longstanding Goal Of Family Reunification.

Although "humanitarian reasons" is not defined either in the Act or the regulations, the term generally connotes a broad range of considerations on which relief may be granted. In fact, as the House Committee indicated, it is to be liberally construed. Early in its administration of the legalization program, the INS had opined that the term "humanitarian" purposes set "a less stringent or restrictive standard than that of the 'extreme hardship' requirement of INA § 212(h)."INS Office of Legalization, draft memorandum, *Waiver on Grounds of Excludability*, CO 1588-C, (August 8, 1987), *reprinted in* 64 Interpreter Releases 930-32 (Aug. 6, 1987).

The lowered threshold is significant, since "extreme hardship" in the 212(h) waiver context has been held to require something beyond minor medical conditions or such common results of the bar to admission as financial difficulty or family separation, standing along. *See Matter of Ngai*, 19 I. & N. Dec. 245 (Comm'r 1984); *cf.Matter of Pao*, File No. A70 270 864 (Comm'r [AAU] (Apr. 23, 1992), *summarized and discussed* at 69 Interpreter Releases 1089, 1094 (Sept. 4, 1992). As a standard for granting suspension of deportation, findings of "extreme hardship" have been made for economic, family, and medical reasons, to be weighed against other factors.

It would stand to reason then, that the same reasons of hardship, without being "extreme," should suffice for reinstatement under the rubric of "humanitarian reasons." Moreover, other significant hardships or difficulties should do as well as situations reasonably calling for benevolence, mercy, or compassion. For instance, recantation of a false statement on an application has been accepted by the Service, as a humanitarian reason for granting a waiver. *See* Letter by Joseph L. Thomas, Director, INS Western Regional Processing Center, Oct. 14, 1987, *reprinted in* 64 Interpreter Releases 1328 (Nov. 23, 1987).

Unlike those seeking certain legalization waivers on humanitarian grounds, Beneficiary in the instant case has neither committed any offenses nor fraud against the United States. Rather, he has waited patiently in Philippines for the processing of his immigrant petition in the past 8 years. But for the unfortunate passing of Petitioner, he would probably be here in United States. Family unity has long been recognized by the courts and Congress as one of the driving forces behind immigration in the United States. As explained by the Ninth Circuit in *Cerrillo-Perez v. INS*,

> *"...It is universally recognized that 'the family is the natural and fundamental group unit of society and is entitled to protection by society and the*

> *state.'Universal Declaration of Human Rights, G.A. Res. 217, U.N. Doc.A/810. According to H.R. Rep. No. 85-1199, 'the legislative history of the Immigration and Nationality Act clearly indicates that the Congress intended to provide for a liberal treatment of children and was concerned with the problem of keeping families of United States citizens and immigrants united." H.R. Rep. No. 1199, 85th Cong., 1st Sess. 7, reprinted in 1957 U.S. Code, Cong. & Admin. News 2016, 2020."*

Cerrillo-Perez v. INS, 809 F.2d 1419, 1423 (9th Cir. 1987). More recently, Congress further reinforced this venerable policy when President Bush signed into law, the Family Sponsor Immigration Act of 2002, effective as of its enactment date on March 13, 2002.

Beneficiary's humanitarian reinstatement should be granted for the compelling interest of family reunification. When Petitioner passed away, Beneficiary essentially lost all hope of being reunited with his brother in the United States. Both Beneficiary and his family pray that he will be allowed to enter the United States.

As mentioned, Beneficiary has been waiting for 8 years for the visa number from his approved I-130 to become current at the U.S. Embassy in Philippines. Beneficiary is already 51-years-old. Moreover, even if his U.S. citizen brother was to file a family petition on his behalf at this point, the visa priority date for Philippines in the category of fourth preference (F4) brothers and sisters of a United States citizen will necessitate a wait of an additional 23 years. *See* https://travel.state.gov/content/visas/en/law-and-policy/bulletin/2017/visa-bulletin-for-august-2017.html. It is highly probable then, that either Beneficiary or his petitioning sibling could pass away before his visa number becomes current again. Consequently, it would appear to fly in the face of Congress' goal of promoting family reunification because of the separation that Beneficiary and his family would be forced to further endure should reinstatement be denied.

C. Beneficiary Has Complied With INA §§ 212(a)(4) And 213A, As Amended By The Family Sponsor Immigration Act Of 2002.

The Family Sponsor Immigration Act of 2002 further reaffirms Congress's commitment to the goal of family reunification in that it, by amending §§ 212(a)(4)(C)(ii) and 213A(f)(5), and remedying the situation of an alien whose petitioner has died following approval of the visa petition but before he or she has obtained permanent residence in the United States.

For cases in which the death of the visa petitioner occurred prior to March 13, 2002 – the date of enactment – the alien must 1) formally request that the Attorney General exercise his or her discretion to reinstate, for humanitarian reasons, the petition that was filed by the deceased petitioner and approved before such death and 2) simultaneously demonstrate that a substitute sponsor exists who meets the standard INA § 213A income requirements and that the substitute sponsor is related to the alien in one of the following ways: as a parent, mother-in-law, father-in-law, sibling, child (if at least 18 years of age), son, daughter, son-in-law, daughter-in-law, sister-in-law, brother-in-law, grandparents, grandchild, or legal guardian (emphasis added). INS Office of the Executive Associate Commissioner, Memorandum for Regional Directors, *Policy Change – Public Law 107-150, the Family Sponsor Immigration Act of 2002: Use of Substitute Sponsor if Visa Petitioner Has Died*, HQADJ 70/21.1.13, (June 15, 2002). In addition, the Executive Associate Commissioner also stated in his memorandum that, reinstatement, while still a matter of discretion, should be "exercised in light of the facts of each individual case, particularly those cases in which failure to reinstate would lead to a harsh result contrary to the goal of family reunification."*Id.*

In present case, Beneficiary's brother is currently residing in the United States. Beneficiary's brother meets the standard under INA § 213A income requirements and is willing and able to step in as the sponsor in lieu of their deceased mother. After having patiently waited for 8 years since his mother initially petitioned him, and now he is 51-year-old, he faces the stark possibility of suffering through 23 more years apart from his family should the Attorney General fail to reinstate the initial approval at this time. Requiring Beneficiary to endure another 23 year of waiting, given the aforementioned circumstances, would be unfair and unjust to the point of being inhumane. Such a result would be diametrically opposed to the magnanimous spirit in which Congress and the President approved the Family Sponsor Immigration Act of 2002.

III. <u>DHS'S CRITERIA IN EVALUATING HUMANITARIAN REINSTATEMENT APPLICATIONS.</u>

A. DHS Criteria In Evaluating A Request For Reinstatement Include:

1. *The impact of revocation on the family unit in the U.S. especially USC/LPR relatives or other relatives living lawfully in the U.S.;*

Beneficiary's brother is the only a family member currently living in the United States. He is a U.S. citizen living alone in San Mateo, California. Beneficiary's brother is suffering from HIV/Aids infection, history of Hepatitis C, Gastro-Oesophageal Reflux disease, Testicular failure with hypogonadism, insomnia, and major depressive disorder recurrent episode and is currently being seen and monitored regularly by a Kaiser specialist doctor Darvin Scott Smith MD and a Psychologist for his depression and anxiety. See **Exhibit 9.** Beneficiary's brother has to take expensive specialty medications daily and for the rest of his life to prevent deterioration of Beneficiary's brother's general health and to keep him alive. Currently, Beneficiary's brother is not a burden to the state government as his health insurance pays for those medications. Since Beneficiary's mother died, Beneficiary's brother has resided in the United States alone. Beneficiary's brother's medical issues are causing emotional depression on him, but he is still working for 40 hours a week as a physical therapist for the sake of his family living in the Philippines. See **Exhibits 1 and 9.**

2. *Beneficiary's advanced age or poor health;*

Beneficiary is already 51-years-old. Beneficiary is worried and gets anxious about his brother's condition since he is living in the United States by himself. Beneficiary's parents already have passed away, and being the oldest in the family, Beneficiary is responsible now for the welfare of his younger brother. Beneficiary would like to reunite with his younger brother because this is his mother's dream for them to live together and support each other in the United States because it is not easy to be alone living in the United States. Building family ties in the United States is very important for them. Beneficiary's brother loved his mother unconditionally. Beneficiary gets emotionally stressed thinking about who can take care of his brother when time comes and he needs help or gets sick but no loved one is there in the United States. Beneficiary feels very sorry and guilty that he cannot be there to be with him during these moments of any emergency. All of them are still suffering from hardship due to the unexpected death of their beloved mother. See **Exhibits 1 and 2.**

3. *Beneficiary's ties to his or her home country;*

Beneficiary has never been married. Beneficiary has his one brother, [redacted] and two sisters [redacted] and [redacted] in the Philippines. However, [redacted] are busy in their world and [redacted]s also filing a similar application for Humanitarian Reinstatement. See **Exhibits 1 and 2.**

IV.
DOS'S CRITERIA IN EVALUATING A REQUEST HUMANITARIAN REINSTATEMENT.

A. As Per DOS's Criteria A Humanitarian Reinstatement Application Should Include The Following Things:

1. *Hardship to USCs or LPRs;*

Beneficiary's brother [redacted] is the only a family member currently living in the United States. He is a U.S. citizen living alone in San Mateo, California. Beneficiary's brother is suffering from HIV/Aids infection, history of Hepatitis C, Gastro-Oesophageal Reflux disease, Testicular failure with hypogonadism, insomnia, and major depressive disorder recurrent episode and is currently being seen and monitored regularly by a Kaiser specialist doctor Darvin Scott Smith MD and a Psychologist for his depression and anxiety. See **Exhibit 9.** Beneficiary's brother has to take expensive specialty medications daily and for the rest of his life to prevent deterioration of his general health and to keep him alive. Currently Beneficiary's brother is not a burden to the state government as his health insurance pays for those medications. He is trying his best to stay emotionally strong for them but, he has to admit it's a daily mental and emotional challenge for him to have a stable mental health and he does not know if he can cope and for how long. His mental health is not as good as before because of the things that happened in his life and he does worry a lot; about his future and his life in general and his family in the Philippines. He loves his family and he will do everything for them. See **Exhibits 1 and 2.**

2. *A beneficiary who is elderly or in poor health;*

Beneficiary is a 53-year-old Filipino lady. See **Exhibit 3.**

3. *A beneficiary who has strong family ties in the U.S. 9 FAM 42.42 PN2. USCIS relies on these same factors.* Sheikh v. DHS, 685 F.Supp.2d 1076, 1090-91 (C.D. Cal. 2010).

Beneficiary's brother has been residing in United States for past 15 years. **Exhibit 2.**

V.
BENEFICIARY IS ALSO ELIGIBLE FOR RELIEF PURSUANT TO SECTION 204(l), HOWEVER, THE ONLY DIFFERENCE IS THAT BENEFICIARY WAS NOT RESIDING IN THE UNITED STATES AT THE TIME OF PETITIONER'S DEATH

A. Eligibility under INA 204(l) Surviving Relative Consideration For Certain Petitions and Applications.

INA section 204(I), which states in pertinent part:

> *204(l)(1) In General.-- An alien described in paragraph (2) who resided in the United States at the time of the death of the qualifying relative and who continues to reside in the United States shall have such petition described in paragraph (2), or an application for adjustment of status to that of a person admitted for lawful permanent residence based upon the family relationship described in paragraph (2), and any related applications, adjudicated notwithstanding the death of the qualifying relative, unless the Secretary of Homeland Security determines, in the unreviewable discretion of the Secretary, that approval would not be in the public interest.*
>
> *(2) Alien Described.-- An alien described in this paragraph is an alien who, immediately prior to the death of his or her qualifying relative, was--*
>
> *(2)(A) the beneficiary of a pending or approved petition for classification as an immediate relative (as described in section 201(b)(2)(A)(i));*

The main requirements are that beneficiary must have been residing in the United States at the time of Petitioner's death and continue to be residing here. The other requirement is that he or she must obtain a substitute sponsor who can file an affidavit of support.

Beneficiary is fulfilling all the condition except one condition i.e. he was not in the United States at the time of Petitioner's death in the United States. However, relief under section 204(l) is not an "entitlement," but a matter that Congress has entrusted to DHS discretion. As with other forms of discretionary relief, exercising discretion means weighing positive factors against negative factors to make a decision. In addition to meeting the basic requirements for section 204(l) relief, your request must warrant a favorable exercise of discretion, meaning that the "pros" in granting your request outweigh the "cons." However, USCIS knows that section 204(l) is intended to help people who were put in an unfortunate position because of a sad event that was beyond their control. The intent of the law is a very strong "pro" factor that weighs favorably in the exercise of discretion.

Therefore, in present case USCIS can Reinstatement under INA § 204(*l*) through its discretionary power.

B. Equal Protection To Beneficiaries Of Approved I-130, Who Are Not Eligible Under Section INA § 204(l).

In present case, Beneficiary is not present in the United States and the relief is only given to those beneficiaries who had resided in the United States at the time of petitioner's death.

Moreover, relief can be availed even if beneficiaries are residing in the United States unlawfully. However, in this case Beneficiary has not violated any immigration laws and should be equally protected as he would be residing in the United States.

VI. CONCLUSION.

Based on the above, Beneficiary respectfully requests that discretion be exercised favorably in granting his request for humanitarian reinstatement so that he may finally be reunited with his family, and that their long wait has not been in vain. Thank you for your kind consideration in this matter.

Sincerely,

Brian D. Lerner
Attorney at Law

SECTION 2:
Forms

Notice of Entry of Appearance as Attorney or Accredited Representative

Department of Homeland Security

DHS Form G-28
OMB No. 1615-0105
Expires 03/31/2018

Part 1. Information About Attorney or Accredited Representative

1. USCIS ELIS Account Number *(if any)* ▶

Name and Address of Attorney or Accredited Representative

2.a. Family Name *(Last Name)*: Lerner
2.b. Given Name *(First Name)*: Brian
2.c. Middle Name: David
3.a. Street Number and Name: 3233 E Broadway
3.b. Apt. ☐ Ste. ☐ Flr. ☐
3.c. City or Town: Long Beach
3.d. State: CA 3.e. ZIP Code: 90803
3.f. Province:
3.g. Postal Code:
3.h. Country: USA
4. Daytime Telephone Number: 5624950554
5. Fax Number: 5626088672
6. E-Mail Address *(if any)*: blerner@californiaimmigration.us
7. Mobile Telephone Number *(if any)*:

Part 2. Notice of Appearance as Attorney or Accredited Representative

This appearance relates to immigration matters before *(Select **only one** box)*:

1.a. ☒ USCIS
1.b. List the form numbers: I-130
2.a. ☐ ICE
2.b. List the specific matter in which appearance is entered:
3.a. ☐ CBP
3.b. List the specific matter in which appearance is entered:

I enter my appearance as attorney or accredited representative at the request of:

4. Select **only one** box:
☒ Applicant ☐ Petitioner ☐ Requestor
☐ Respondent (ICE, CBP)

Information About Applicant, Petitioner, Requestor, or Respondent

5.a. Family Name *(Last Name)*: [redacted]
5.b. Given Name *(First Name)*: [redacted]
5.c. Middle Name: [redacted]
6. Name of Company or Organization *(if applicable)*:

Part 2. Notice of Appearance as Attorney or Accredited Representative *(continued)*

Information About Applicant, Petitioner, Requestor, or Respondent (continued)

7. USCIS ELIS Account Number *(if any)*

▶

8. Alien Registration Number (A-Number) or Receipt Number

WAC0907614030

9. Daytime Telephone Number

10. Mobile Telephone Number *(if any)*

11. E-Mail Address *(if any)*

Mailing Address of Applicant, Petitioner, Requestor, or Respondent

NOTE: Provide the mailing address of the applicant, petitioner, requestor, or respondent. **Do not** provide the business mailing address of the attorney or accredited representative **unless** it serves as the safe mailing address on the application, petition, or request being filed with this Form G-28.

12.a. Street Number and Name

12.b. Apt. [X] Ste. [ ] Flr. [ ]

12.c. City or Town

12.d. State 12.e. ZIP Code

12.f. Province

12.g. Postal Code

12.h. Country

USA

Part 3. Eligibility Information for Attorney or Accredited Representative

Select **all applicable** items.

1.a. [X] I am an attorney eligible to practice law in, and a member in good standing of, the bar of the highest courts of the following states, possessions, territories, commonwealths, or the District of Columbia. *(If you need additional space, use **Part 6.**)*

Licensing Authority

Supreme Court of California

1.b. Bar Number *(if applicable)*

158536

1.c. Name of Law Firm

Law Offices of Brian D. Lerner

1.d. I *(choose one)* [X] ***am not*** [ ] ***am***

subject to any order of any court or administrative agency disbarring, suspending, enjoining, restraining, or otherwise restricting me in the practice of law. If you are subject to any orders, explain in the space below. *(If you need additional space, use **Part 6.**)*

2.a. [ ] I am an accredited representative of the following qualified nonprofit religious, charitable, social service, or similar organization established in the United States, so recognized by the Department of Justice, Board of Immigration Appeals, in accordance with 8 CFR 292.2. Provide the name of the organization and the expiration date of accreditation.

2.b. Name of Recognized Organization

2.c. Date accreditation expires

(mm/dd/yyyy) ▶

Part 3. Eligibility Information for Attorney or Accredited Representative *(continued)*

3. ☐ I am associated with [ ], the attorney or accredited representative of record who previously filed Form G-28 in this case, and my appearance as an attorney or accredited representative is at his or her request.

NOTE: If you select this item, also complete **Item Numbers 1.a. - 1.b. or Item Numbers 2.a. - 2.c.** in **Part 3.** *(whichever is appropriate).*

4.a. ☐ I am a law student or law graduate working under the direct supervision of the attorney or accredited representative of record on this form in accordance with the requirements in 8 CFR 292.1(a)(2)(iv).

4.b. Name of Law Student or Law Graduate

Part 4. Applicant, Petitioner, Requestor, or Respondent Consent to Representation, Contact Information, and Signature

Consent to Representation and Release of Information

1. I have requested the representation of and consented to being represented by the attorney or accredited representative named in **Part 1.** of this form. According to the Privacy Act of 1974 and DHS policy, I also consent to the disclosure to the named attorney or accredited representative of any record pertaining to me that appears in any system of records of USCIS, ICE or CBP.

When you (the applicant, petitioner, requestor, or respondent) are represented, DHS will send notices to both you and your attorney or accredited representative either through mail or electronic delivery.

DHS will also send the Form I-94, Arrival Departure Record, to you **unless** you select **Item Number 2.a.** in **Part 4.** All secure identity documents and Travel Documents will be sent to you (the applicant, petitioner, requestor, or respondent) at your U.S. mailing address **unless** you ask us to send your secure identity documents to your attorney of record or accredited representative.

If you do not want to receive original notices or secure identity documents directly, but would rather have such notices and documents sent to your attorney of record or accredited representative, please select **all applicable** boxes below:

2.a ☒ I request DHS send any notice (including Form I-94) on an application, petition, or request to the U.S. business address of my attorney of record or accredited representative as listed in this form. I understand that I may change this election at any future date through written notice to DHS.

2.b. ☐ I request that DHS send any secure identity document, such as a Permanent Resident Card, Employment Authorization Document, or Travel Document, that I am approved to receive and authorized to possess, to the U.S. business address of my attorney of record or accredited representative as listed in this form or to a designated military or diplomatic address for pickup in a foreign country (if permitted). I consent to having my secure identity document sent to my attorney of record or accredited representative's U.S. business address and understand that I may request, at any future date and through written notice to DHS, that DHS send any secure identity document to me directly.

3.a. Signature of Applicant, Petitioner, Requestor, or Respondent

3.b. Date of Signature *(mm/dd/yyyy)* ► 09-14-2017

Part 5. Signature of Attorney or Accredited Representative

I have read and understand the regulations and conditions contained in 8 CFR 103.2 and 292 governing appearances and representation before the Department of Homeland Security. I declare under penalty of perjury under the laws of the United States that the information I have provided on this form is true and correct.

1. Signature of Attorney or Accredited Representative

2. Signature of Law Student or Law Graduate

3. Date of Signature *(mm/dd/yyyy)* ►

Part 6. Additional Information

Use the space provided below to provide additional information pertaining to **Part 3., Item Numbers 1.a. - 1.d.** or to provide your U.S. business address for purposes of receiving secure identity documents for your client (if your client has consented to your receipt of such documents under **Part 4.**)

Notice of Entry of Appearance as Attorney or Accredited Representative

Department of Homeland Security

DHS Form G-28
OMB No. 1615-0105
Expires 03/31/2018

Part 1. Information About Attorney or Accredited Representative

1. USCIS ELIS Account Number *(if any)* ▶

Name and Address of Attorney or Accredited Representative

2.a. Family Name *(Last Name)* Lerner
2.b. Given Name *(First Name)* Brian
2.c. Middle Name David
3.a. Street Number and Name 3233 E Broadway
3.b. Apt. ☐ Ste. ☐ Flr. ☐
3.c. City or Town Long Beach
3.d. State CA 3.e. ZIP Code 90803
3.f. Province
3.g. Postal Code
3.h. Country USA
4. Daytime Telephone Number 5624950554
5. Fax Number 5626088672
6. E-Mail Address *(if any)* blerner@californiaimmigration.us
7. Mobile Telephone Number *(if any)*

Part 2. Notice of Appearance as Attorney or Accredited Representative

This appearance relates to immigration matters before *(Select **only one** box)*:

1.a. ☒ USCIS
1.b. List the form numbers I-864
2.a. ☐ ICE
2.b. List the specific matter in which appearance is entered
3.a. ☐ CBP
3.b. List the specific matter in which appearance is entered

I enter my appearance as attorney or accredited representative at the request of:

4. Select **only one** box:
☐ Applicant ☒ Petitioner ☐ Requestor
☐ Respondent (ICE, CBP)

Information About Applicant, Petitioner, Requestor, or Respondent

5.a. Family Name *(Last Name)* [redacted]
5.b. Given Name *(First Name)* [redacted]
5.c. Middle Name [redacted]
6. Name of Company or Organization *(if applicable)*

Part 2. Notice of Appearance as Attorney or Accredited Representative *(continued)*

Information About Applicant, Petitioner, Requestor, or Respondent (continued)

7. USCIS ELIS Account Number *(if any)*
▶

8. Alien Registration Number (A-Number) or Receipt Number

9. Daytime Telephone Number

10. Mobile Telephone Number *(if any)*

11. E-Mail Address *(if any)*

Mailing Address of Applicant, Petitioner, Requestor, or Respondent

NOTE: Provide the mailing address of the applicant, petitioner, requestor, or respondent. **Do not** provide the business mailing address of the attorney or accredited representative **unless** it serves as the safe mailing address on the application, petition, or request being filed with this Form G-28.

12.a. Street Number and Name [redacted]

12.b. Apt. ☒ Ste. ☐ Flr. ☐ [redacted]

12.c. City or Town [redacted]

12.d. State [redacted] 12.e. ZIP Code [redacted]

12.f. Province

12.g. Postal Code

12.h. Country
USA

Part 3. Eligibility Information for Attorney or Accredited Representative

Select **all applicable** items.

1.a. ☒ I am an attorney eligible to practice law in, and a member in good standing of, the bar of the highest courts of the following states, possessions, territories, commonwealths, or the District of Columbia. *(If you need additional space, use* ***Part 6.****)*

Licensing Authority
Supreme Court of California

1.b. Bar Number *(if applicable)*
158536

1.c. Name of Law Firm
Law Offices of Brian D. Lerner

1.d. I *(choose one)* ☒ ***am not*** ☐ ***am***
subject to any order of any court or administrative agency disbarring, suspending, enjoining, restraining, or otherwise restricting me in the practice of law. If you are subject to any orders, explain in the space below. *(If you need additional space, use* ***Part 6.****)*

2.a. ☐ I am an accredited representative of the following qualified nonprofit religious, charitable, social service, or similar organization established in the United States, so recognized by the Department of Justice, Board of Immigration Appeals, in accordance with 8 CFR 292.2. Provide the name of the organization and the expiration date of accreditation.

2.b. Name of Recognized Organization

2.c. Date accreditation expires
(mm/dd/yyyy) ▶

Part 3. Eligibility Information for Attorney or Accredited Representative *(continued)*

3. ☐ I am associated with [blank], the attorney or accredited representative of record who previously filed Form G-28 in this case, and my appearance as an attorney or accredited representative is at his or her request.

NOTE: If you select this item, also complete **Item Numbers 1.a. - 1.b. or Item Numbers 2.a. - 2.c.** in **Part 3.** *(whichever is appropriate).*

4.a. ☐ I am a law student or law graduate working under the direct supervision of the attorney or accredited representative of record on this form in accordance with the requirements in 8 CFR 292.1(a)(2)(iv).

4.b. Name of Law Student or Law Graduate

Part 4. Applicant, Petitioner, Requestor, or Respondent Consent to Representation, Contact Information, and Signature

Consent to Representation and Release of Information

1. I have requested the representation of and consented to being represented by the attorney or accredited representative named in **Part 1.** of this form. According to the Privacy Act of 1974 and DHS policy, I also consent to the disclosure to the named attorney or accredited representative of any record pertaining to me that appears in any system of records of USCIS, ICE or CBP.

When you (the applicant, petitioner, requestor, or respondent) are represented, DHS will send notices to both you and your attorney or accredited representative either through mail or electronic delivery.

DHS will also send the Form I-94, Arrival Departure Record, to you **unless** you select **Item Number 2.a.** in **Part 4.** All secure identity documents and Travel Documents will be sent to you (the applicant, petitioner, requestor, or respondent) at your U.S. mailing address **unless** you ask us to send your secure identity documents to your attorney of record or accredited representative.

If you do not want to receive original notices or secure identity documents directly, but would rather have such notices and documents sent to your attorney of record or accredited representative, please select **all applicable** boxes below:

2.a ☒ I request DHS send any notice (including Form I-94) on an application, petition, or request to the U.S. business address of my attorney of record or accredited representative as listed in this form. I understand that I may change this election at any future date through written notice to DHS.

2.b. ☐ I request that DHS send any secure identity document, such as a Permanent Resident Card, Employment Authorization Document, or Travel Document, that I am approved to receive and authorized to possess, to the U.S. business address of my attorney of record or accredited representative as listed in this form or to a designated military or diplomatic address for pickup in a foreign country (if permitted). I consent to having my secure identity document sent to my attorney of record or accredited representative's U.S. business address and understand that I may request, at any future date and through written notice to DHS, that DHS send any secure identity document to me directly.

3.a. Signature of Applicant, Petitioner, Requestor, or Respondent

➡ [signature redacted]

3.b. Date of Signature *(mm/dd/yyyy)*▶ 9/7/17

Part 5. Signature of Attorney or Accredited Representative

I have read and understand the regulations and conditions contained in 8 CFR 103.2 and 292 governing appearances and representation before the Department of Homeland Security. I declare under penalty of perjury under the laws of the United States that the information I have provided on this form is true and correct.

1. Signature of Attorney or Accredited Representative [signature]

2. Signature of Law Student or Law Graduate

3. Date of Signature *(mm/dd/yyyy)*▶

Part 6. Additional Information

Use the space provided below to provide additional information pertaining to **Part 3., Item Numbers 1.a. - 1.d.** or to provide your U.S. business address for purposes of receiving secure identity documents for your client (if your client has consented to your receipt of such documents under **Part 4.**)

Affidavit of Support Under Section 213A of the INA

Department of Homeland Security
U.S. Citizenship and Immigration Services

USCIS Form I-864
OMB No. 1615-0075
Expires 07/31/2017

For USCIS Use Only	Affidavit of Support Submitter	Section 213A Review	Number of Support Affidavits in File
	☐ Petitioner ☐ 1st Joint Sponsor ☐ 2nd Joint Sponsor ☐ Substitute Sponsor ☐ 5% Owner	☐ MEETS requirements ☐ DOES NOT MEET requirements Reviewed By: ______ Office: ______ Date (mm/dd/yyyy): ______	☐ 1 ☐ 2 Remarks

► **START HERE - Type or print in black ink.**

Part 1. Basis For Filing Affidavit of Support

I, [redacted], am the sponsor submitting this affidavit of support because (Select **only one** box):

1.a. ☐ I am the petitioner. I filed or am filing for the immigration of my relative.

1.b. ☐ I filed an alien worker petition on behalf of the intending immigrant, who is related to me as my ______

1.c. ☐ I have an ownership interest of at least 5 percent in ______ which filed an alien worker petition on behalf of the intending immigrant, who is related to me as my ______

1.d. ☐ I am the only joint sponsor.

1.e. ☐ I am the ☐ first ☐ second of two joint sponsors.

1.f. ☒ The original petitioner is deceased. I am the substitute sponsor. I am the intending immigrant's Sibling

NOTE: If you select Item Number 1.a., 1.b., 1.c., 1.d., 1.e., or 1.f., you must include proof of your U.S. citizenship, U.S. national status, or lawful permanent resident status.

Part 2. Information About the Principal Immigrant

1.a. Family Name (Last Name) [redacted]

1.b. Given Name (First Name) [redacted]

1.c. Middle Name [redacted]

Mailing Address

2.a. In Care Of Name [redacted]

2.b. Street Number and Name [redacted]

2.c. ☒ Apt. ☐ Ste. ☐ Flr. [redacted]

2.d. City or Town [redacted]

2.e. State [redacted] **2.f.** ZIP Code [redacted]

2.g. Province

2.h. Postal Code

2.i. Country USA

Part 2. Information About the Principal Immigrant (continued)

Other Information

3. Country of Citizenship or Nationality
Philippines

4. Date of Birth (mm/dd/yyyy) 02/19/1966

5. Alien Registration Number (A-Number) (if any)
► A-

6. USCIS ELIS Account Number (if any)
►

7. Daytime Telephone Number

Part 3. Information About the Immigrants You Are Sponsoring

1. I am sponsoring the principal immigrant named in **Part 2.**
[X] Yes [ ] No (Applicable only if you are sponsoring family members in **Part 3.** as the second joint sponsor)

2. [ ] I am sponsoring the following family members immigrating at the same time or within six months of the principal immigrant named in **Part 2.** (Do not include any relative listed on a separate visa petition.)

Family Member 1

3.a. Family Name (Last Name)

3.b. Given Name (First Name)

3.c. Middle Name

4. Relationship to Sponsored Immigrant

5. Date of Birth (mm/dd/yyyy)

6. Alien Registration Number (A-Number) (if any)
► A-

7. USCIS ELIS Account Number (if any)
►

Family Member 2

8.a. Family Name (Last Name)

8.b. Given Name (First Name)

8.c. Middle Name

9. Relationship to Sponsored Immigrant

10. Date of Birth (mm/dd/yyyy)

11. Alien Registration Number (A-Number) (if any)
► A-

12. USCIS ELIS Account Number (if any)
►

Family Member 3

13.a. Family Name (Last Name)

13.b. Given Name (First Name)

13.c. Middle Name

14. Relationship to Sponsored Immigrant

15. Date of Birth (mm/dd/yyyy)

16. Alien Registration Number (A-Number) (if any)
► A-

17. USCIS ELIS Account Number (if any)
►

Family Member 4

18.a. Family Name (Last Name)

18.b. Given Name (First Name)

18.c. Middle Name

Part 3. Information About the Immigrants You Are Sponsoring (continued)

19. Relationship to Sponsored Immigrant

20. Date of Birth (mm/dd/yyyy)

21. Alien Registration Number (A-Number) (if any)
► A-

22. USCIS ELIS Account Number (if any)
►

Family Member 5

23.a. Family Name (Last Name)

23.b. Given Name (First Name)

23.c. Middle Name

24. Relationship to Sponsored Immigrant

25. Date of Birth (mm/dd/yyyy)

26. Alien Registration Number (A-Number) (if any)
► A-

27. USCIS ELIS Account Number (if any)
►

28. Enter the total number of immigrants you are sponsoring on this affidavit from **Item Numbers 1.a. - 27.**
1

Part 4. Information About You (Sponsor)

Sponsor's Full Name

1.a. Family Name (Last Name) [redacted]

1.b. Given Name (First Name) [redacted]

1.c. Middle Name [redacted]

Sponsor's Mailing Address

2.a. In Care Of Name [redacted]

2.b. Street Number and Name [redacted]

2.c. ☒ Apt. ☐ Ste. ☐ Flr. [redacted]

2.d. City or Town [redacted]

2.e. State [redacted] 2.f. ZIP Code [redacted]

2.g. Province

2.h. Postal Code

2.i. Country
USA

3. Is your current mailing address the same as your physical address? ☒ Yes ☐ No

If you answered "No" to **Item Number 3.**, provide your physical address below.

Sponsor's Physical Address

4.a. Street Number and Name

4.b. ☐ Apt. ☐ Ste. ☐ Flr.

4.c. City or Town

4.d. State 4.e. ZIP Code

4.f. Province

4.g. Postal Code

4.h. Country

For USCIS Use Only

Part 4. Information About You (Sponsor) (continued)

Other Information

5. Country of Domicile
USA

6. Date of Birth (mm/dd/yyyy) 08/06/1971

7. City or Town of Birth
Manila

8. State or Province of Birth

9. Country of Birth
Philippines

10. U.S. Social Security Number (Required)
► [redacted]

Citizenship or Residency

11.a. [X] I am a U.S. citizen.

11.b. [ ] I am a U.S. national.

11.c. [ ] I am a lawful permanent resident.

12. Sponsor's A-Number (if any)
► A- [redacted]

13. Sponsor's USCIS ELIS Account Number (if any)
►

Military Service (To be completed by petitioner sponsors only.)

14. I am currently on **active duty** in the U.S. Armed Forces or U.S. Coast Guard. [ ] Yes [X] No

Part 5. Sponsor's Household Size

NOTE: Do not count any member of your household more than once.

Persons you are sponsoring in this affidavit:

1. Provide the number you entered in **Part 3., Item Number 28.** 1

Persons NOT sponsored in this affidavit:

2. Yourself. 1

3. If you are currently married, enter "1" for your spouse.

4. If you have dependent children, enter the number here.

5. If you have any other dependents, enter the number here. 1

6. If you have sponsored any other persons on Form I-864 or Form I-864 EZ who are now lawful permanent residents, enter the number here.

7. **OPTIONAL:** If you have siblings, parents, or adult children with the same principal residence who are combining their income with yours by submitting Form I-864A, enter the number here.

8. Add together **Part 5., Item Numbers 1. - 7.** and enter the number here. **Household Size:** 3

For USCIS Use Only

Part 6. Sponsor's Employment and Income

I am currently:

1.a. [X] Employed as a/an

Travelling Physical Therapist

1.a.1. Name of Employer 1 (if applicable)

Harden Home Health

1.a.2. Name of Employer 2 (if applicable)

Calcare Home Health Care

1.b. [ ] Self employed as a/an (Occupation)

1.c. [ ] Retired From (Company Name)

since (mm/dd/yyyy)

1.d. [ ] Unemployed

since (mm/dd/yyyy)

2. My current individual annual income is:

$ 54782

Income you are using from any other person who was counted in your household size, including, in certain conditions, the intending immigrant. (See Form I-864 Instructions.) Please indicate name, relationship, and income.

Person 1

3. Name

4. Relationship

5. **Current Income** $

Person 2

6. Name

7. Relationship

8. **Current Income** $

Person 3

9. Name

10. Relationship

11. **Current Income** $

Person 4

12. Name

13. Relationship

14. **Current Income** $

15. **My Current Annual Household Income** (Total all lines from **Part 6., Item Numbers 2., 5., 8., 11., and 14.**; the total will be compared to Federal Poverty Guidelines on Form I-864P.) $ 54782

16. [ ] The people listed in **Item Numbers 3., 6., 9., and 12.** have completed Form I-864A. I am filing along with this affidavit all necessary Form I-864As completed by these people.

For USCIS Use Only	Household Size	Poverty Guideline	Remarks
	☐ 1 ☐ 2 ☐ 3 ☐ 4 ☐ 5 ☐ 6 ☐ 7 ☐ 8 ☐ 9 ☐ Other______	Year: 2 0 ____ Poverty Line: $__________	

Part 6. Sponsor's Employment and Income (continued)

17. ☐ One or more of the people listed in **Item Numbers 3., 6., 9.,** and **12.** do not need to complete Form I-864A because he or she is the intending immigrant and has no accompanying dependents.

Name

Federal Income Tax Return Information

18.a. Have you filed a Federal income tax return for each of the three most recent tax years? ☒ Yes ☐ No

NOTE: You **MUST** attach a photocopy or transcript of your Federal income tax return for only the most recent tax year.

18.b. ☐ (Optional) I have attached photocopies or transcripts of my Federal income tax returns for my second and third most recent tax years.

My total income (adjusted gross income on Internal Revenue Service (IRS) Form 1040EZ) as reported on my Federal income tax returns for the most recent three years was:

	Tax Year		Total Income
19.a. Most Recent	2016	$	54782
19.b. 2nd Most Recent	2015	$	56482
19.c. 3rd Most Recent	2014	$	125008

20. ☐ I was not required to file a Federal income tax return as my income was below the IRS required level and I have attached evidence to support this.

Part 7. Use of Assets to Supplement Income (Optional)

If your income, or the total income for you and your household, from Part 6., Item Numbers 19.a. - 19.c., exceeds the Federal Poverty Guidelines for your household size, YOU ARE NOT REQUIRED to complete this Part 7. Skip to Part 8.

Your Assets (Optional)

1. Enter the balance of all savings and checking accounts. $

2. Enter the net cash value of real-estate holdings. (Net value means current assessed value minus mortgage debt.) $

3. Enter the net cash value of all stocks, bonds, certificates of deposit, and any other assets not already included in **Item Number 1.** or **Item Number 2.** $

4. **Add together Item Numbers 1. - 3. and enter the number here.** **TOTAL:** $

Assets from Form I-864A, Part 4., Item Number 3.d., for:

5.a. Name of Relative

5.b. Your household member's assets from Form I-864A (optional). $

Assets of the principal sponsored immigrant (optional). The principal sponsored immigrant is the person listed in **Part 2., Item Numbers 1.a. - 1.c.**

6. Enter the balance of the sponsored immigrant's savings and checking accounts. $

For USCIS Use Only	Household Size	Poverty Guideline	Sponsor's Household Income (Page 5, Line 10)	Remarks
	☐ 1 ☐ 2 ☐ 3 ☐ 4 ☐ 5 ☐ 6 ☐ 7 ☐ 8 ☐ 9 ☐ Other______	Year: 20____ Poverty Line: $______	$______	
			The total value of all assets, line 10, must equal 5 times (3 times for spouses and children of USC's, or 1 time for orphans to be formally adopted in the U.S.) the difference between the poverty guidelines and the sponsor's household income, line 10.	

Part 7. Use of Assets to Supplement Income (Optional) (continued)

7. Enter the net cash value of all the sponsored immigrant's real estate holdings. (Net value means investment value minus mortgage debt.) $______

8. Enter the current cash value of the sponsored immigrant's stocks, bonds, certificates of deposit, and other assets not included in **Item Number 6.** or **Item Number 7.** $______

9. **Add together Item Numbers 6. - 8. and enter the number here.** $______

Total Value of Assets

10. **Add together Item Numbers 4., 5.b., and 9. and enter the number here. TOTAL:** $______

Part 8. Sponsor's Contract, Statement, Contact Information, Certification, and Signature

NOTE: Read the information on penalties in the **Penalties** section of the Form I-864 Instructions before completing this part.

Sponsor's Contract

Please note that, by signing this Form I-864, you agree to assume certain specific obligations under the Immigration and Nationality Act (INA) and other Federal laws. The following paragraphs describe those obligations. Please read the following information carefully before you sign Form I-864. If you do not understand the obligations, you may wish to consult an attorney or accredited representative.

What is the Legal Effect of My Signing Form I-864?

If you sign Form I-864 on behalf of any person (called the intending immigrant) who is applying for an immigrant visa or for adjustment of status to a lawful permanent resident, and that intending immigrant submits Form I-864 to the U.S. Government with his or her application for an immigrant visa or adjustment of status, under INA section 213A, these actions create a contract between you and the U.S. Government. The intending immigrant becoming a lawful permanent resident is the consideration for the contract.

Under this contract, you agree that, in deciding whether the intending immigrant can establish that he or she is not inadmissible to the United States as a person likely to become a public charge, the U.S. Government can consider your income and assets as available for the support of the intending immigrant.

What If I Choose Not to Sign Form I-864?

The U.S. Government cannot make you sign Form I-864 if you do not want to do so. But if you do not sign Form I-864, the intending immigrant may not become a lawful permanent resident in the United States.

What Does Signing Form I-864 Require Me to do?

If an intending immigrant becomes a lawful permanent resident in the United States based on a Form I-864 that you have signed, then, until your obligations under Form I-864 terminate, you must:

A. Provide the intending immigrant any support necessary to maintain him or her at an income that is at least 125 percent of the Federal Poverty Guidelines for his or her household size (100 percent if you are the petitioning sponsor and are on active duty in the U.S. Armed Forces or U.S. Coast Guard, and the person is your husband, wife, or unmarried child under 21 years of age); and

Part 8. Sponsor's Contract, Statement, Contact Information, Certification, and Signature (continued)

B. Notify U.S. Citizenship and Immigration Services (USCIS) of any change in your address, within 30 days of the change, by filing Form I-865.

What Other Consequences Are There?

If an intending immigrant becomes a lawful permanent resident in the United States based on a Form I-864 that you have signed, then, until your obligations under Form I-864 terminate, the U.S. Government may consider (deem) your income and assets as available to that person, in determining whether he or she is eligible for certain Federal means-tested public benefits and also for state or local means-tested public benefits, if the state or local government's rules provide for consideration (deeming) of your income and assets as available to the person.

This provision does **not** apply to public benefits specified in section 403(c) of the Welfare Reform Act such as emergency Medicaid, short-term, non-cash emergency relief; services provided under the National School Lunch and Child Nutrition Acts; immunizations and testing and treatment for communicable diseases; and means-tested programs under the Elementary and Secondary Education Act.

What If I Do Not Fulfill My Obligations?

If you do not provide sufficient support to the person who becomes a lawful permanent resident based on a Form I-864 that you signed, that person may sue you for this support.

If a Federal, state, local, or private agency provided any covered means-tested public benefit to the person who becomes a lawful permanent resident based on a Form I-864 that you signed, the agency may ask you to reimburse them for the amount of the benefits they provided. If you do not make the reimbursement, the agency may sue you for the amount that the agency believes you owe.

If you are sued, and the court enters a judgment against you, the person or agency that sued you may use any legally permitted procedures for enforcing or collecting the judgment. You may also be required to pay the costs of collection, including attorney fees.

If you do not file a properly completed Form I-865 within 30 days of any change of address, USCIS may impose a civil fine for your failing to do so.

When Will These Obligations End?

Your obligations under a Form I-864 that you signed will end if the person who becomes a lawful permanent resident based on that affidavit:

A. Becomes a U.S. citizen;

B. Has worked, or can receive credit for, 40 quarters of coverage under the Social Security Act;

C. No longer has lawful permanent resident status and has departed the United States;

D. Is subject to removal, but applies for and obtains, in removal proceedings, a new grant of adjustment of status, based on a new affidavit of support, if one is required; or

E. Dies.

NOTE: Divorce **does not** terminate your obligations under Form I-864.

Your obligations under a Form I-864 that you signed also end if you die. Therefore, if you die, your estate is not required to take responsibility for the person's support after your death. However, your estate may owe any support that you accumulated before you died.

Sponsor's Statement

NOTE: Select the box for either **Item Number 1.a.** or **1.b.** If applicable, select the box for **Item Number 2.**

1.a. ☐ I can read and understand English, and have read and understand every question and instruction on this affidavit, as well as my answer to every question.

1.b. ☐ The interpreter named in **Part 9.** has also read to me every question and instruction on this affidavit, as well as my answer to every question, in ______________________, a language in which I am fluent. I understand every question and instruction on this affidavit as translated to me by my interpreter, and have provided complete, true, and correct responses in the language indicated above.

Part 8. Sponsor's Contract, Statement, Contact Information, Certification, and Signature (continued)

2. [X] I have requested the services of and consented to Brian D Lerner, who [X] is [ ] is not an attorney or accredited representative, preparing this affidavit for me.

Sponsor's Contact Information

3. Sponsor's Daytime Telephone Number

4. Sponsor's Mobile Telephone Number (if any)

5. Sponsor's Email Address (if any)

Sponsor's Certification

Copies of any documents I have submitted are exact photocopies of unaltered, original documents, and I understand that USCIS or the Department of State may require that I submit original documents to USCIS or the Department of State at a later date. Furthermore, I authorize the release of any information from any and all of my records that USCIS or the Department of State may need to determine my eligibility for the benefit that I seek.

I furthermore authorize release of information contained in this affidavit, in supporting documents, and in my USCIS or Department of State records to other entities and persons where necessary for the administration and enforcement of U.S. immigration laws.

I certify, under penalty of perjury, that the information in my affidavit and any document submitted with my affidavit were provided by me and are complete, true, and correct, and:

A. I know the contents of this affidavit of support that I signed;

B. I have read and I understand each of the obligations described in **Part 8.**, and I agree, freely and without any mental reservation or purpose of evasion, to accept each of those obligations in order to make it possible for the immigrants indicated in **Part 3.** to become lawful permanent residents of the United States;

C. I agree to submit to the personal jurisdiction of any Federal or state court that has subject matter jurisdiction of a lawsuit against me to enforce my obligations under this Form I-864;

D. Each of the Federal income tax returns submitted in support of this affidavit are true copies, or are unaltered tax transcripts, of the tax returns I filed with the IRS;

E. I understand that, if I am related to the sponsored immigrant by marriage, the termination of the marriage (by divorce, dissolution, annulment, or other legal process) will not relieve me of my obligations under this Form I-864; and

F. I authorize the Social Security Administration to release information about me in its records to the Department of State and USCIS.

Sponsor's Signature

6.a. Sponsor's Signature

6.b. Date of Signature (mm/dd/yyyy) 9/7/17

NOTE TO ALL SPONSORS: If you do not completely fill out this affidavit or fail to submit required documents listed in the Instructions, USCIS or the Department of State may deny your affidavit.

Part 9. Interpreter's Contact Information, Certification, and Signature

Provide the following information about the interpreter.

Interpreter's Full Name

1.a. Interpreter's Family Name (Last Name)

1.b. Interpreter's Given Name (First Name)

2. Interpreter's Business or Organization Name (if any)

Interpreter's Mailing Address

3.a. Street Number and Name

3.b. ☐ Apt. ☐ Ste. ☐ Flr.

3.c. City or Town

3.d. State **3.e.** ZIP Code

3.f. Province

3.g. Postal Code

3.h. Country

Interpreter's Contact Information

4. Interpreter's Daytime Telephone Number

5. Interpreter's Email Address (if any)

Interpreter's Certification

I certify that:

I am fluent in English and __________, which is the same language provided in **Part 8., Item Number 1.b.**;

I have read to this sponsor every question and instruction on this affidavit, as well as the answer to every question, in the language provided in **Part 8., Item Number 1.b.**; and

The sponsor has informed me that he or she understands every instruction and question on the affidavit, as well as the answer to every question, and the sponsor verified the accuracy of every answer.

Interpreter's Signature

6.a. Interpreter's Signature

6.b. Date of Signature (mm/dd/yyyy)

Part 10. Contact Information, Statement, Certification, and Signature of the Person Preparing this Affidavit, If Other Than the Sponsor

Provide the following information about the preparer.

Preparer's Full Name

1.a. Preparer's Family Name (Last Name)
Lerner

1.b. Preparer's Given Name (First Name)
Brian

2. Preparer's Business or Organization Name (if any)
Law Offices of Brian D. Lerner

Part 10. Contact Information, Statement, Certification, and Signature of the Person Preparing this Affidavit, If Other Than the Sponsor (continued)

Preparer's Mailing Address

3.a. Street Number and Name: 3233 E Broadway

3.b. ☐ Apt. ☐ Ste. ☐ Flr.

3.c. City or Town: Long Beach

3.d. State: CA 3.e. ZIP Code: 90803

3.f. Province:

3.g. Postal Code:

3.h. Country: USA

Preparer's Contact Information

4. Preparer's Daytime Telephone Number: 5624950554

5. Preparer's Fax Number: 5626088672

6. Preparer's Email Address (if any): blerner@californiaimmigration.us

Preparer's Statement

7.a. ☐ I am not an attorney or accredited representative but have prepared this affidavit on behalf of the sponsor and with the sponsor's consent.

7.b. ☒ I am an attorney or accredited representative and my representation of the sponsor in this case ☒ extends ☐ does not extend beyond the preparation of this affidavit.

NOTE: If you are an attorney or accredited representative whose representation extends beyond preparation of this affidavit, you must submit a completed Form G-28, Notice of Entry of Appearance as Attorney or Accredited Representative, with this affidavit.

Preparer's Certification

By my signature, I certify, swear, or affirm, under penalty of perjury, that I prepared this affidavit on behalf of, at the request of, and with the express consent of the sponsor. I completed this affidavit based only on responses the sponsor provided to me. After completing the affidavit, I reviewed it and all of the responses with the sponsor, who agreed with every answer on the affidavit. If the sponsor supplied additional information concerning a question on the affidavit, I recorded it on the affidavit.

Preparer's Signature

8.a. Preparer's Signature: [signature]

8.b. Date of Signature (mm/dd/yyyy):

Part 11. Additional Information

If you need extra space to provide any additional information within this affidavit, use the space below. If you need more space than what is provided, you may make copies of this page to complete and file with this affidavit or attach a separate sheet of paper. Include your name and A-Number (if any) at the top of each sheet; indicate the **Page Number, Part Number,** and **Item Number** to which your answer refers; and sign and date each sheet.

Your Full Name

1.a. Family Name (Last Name) [redacted]

1.b. Given Name (First Name) [redacted]

1.c. Middle Name [redacted]

2. A-Number (if any)
► A- [redacted]

3.a. Page Number 3.b. Part Number 3.c. Item Number

3.d.

4.a. Page Number 4.b. Part Number 4.c. Item Number

4.d.

5.a. Page Number 5.b. Part Number 5.c. Item Number

5.d.

SECTION 3:
Exhibits

Exhibit 1:

Declaration of Beneficiary

I,] hereby declare as follows:

1. I have personal knowledge of all the facts contained in this declaration, and if called upon to testify I would do so.

2. I reside in Cavite, Philippines.

3. I was born on February 19, 1966 in Manila, Philippines. I am a citizen of the Philippines. On December 18, 2008, my U.S. citizen mother, filed an I-130, Petition for Alien, on my behalf pursuant to INA § 203(a)(2)(B), which was approved on November 19, 2009. Unfortunately, my mother died on June 28, 2013.

4. I have two younger brothers; 46-year-old who is a U.S. citizen through Naturalization, and 50-year-old who is a citizen of Philippines, and two sisters, 53-year-old who is a citizen of Philippines and 48-year-old , who is a citizen of Philippines.

5. My brother, who lives in California, is single and has never been married. He is a hard working professional Physical Therapist. , me and my other sister want to reunite and live in the United States, to fulfill my mother's wish for us to take care of each other in the United States. I have never been in the United States.

6. My younger brother is the only family member currently living in the United States. My brother is suffering from major depression and anxiety and currently undergoing medical testing and counseling due to the death of our mother in 2013. He is suffering from HIV/Aids infection, history of Hepatitis C, Gastro-Oesophageal Reflux disease, Testicular failure with hypogonadism, insomnia, and major depressive disorder recurrent episode. It will be a big help emotionally if we can all live together in the United States so that we can support each other. My biggest hardship is the prolonged separation from my brother Jose; he has been helping us for many years. If I am unable to immigrate to United States, I will suffer emotional hardship. Every day I will be worried and get anxious about my brother's health and mental condition since he is living there by himself.

7. Both of my parents had already passed away; I am responsible now for the welfare of my beloved younger brother. I would like to reunite with my younger brother because this is my mother's dream for us all to live together and support each other in the United States. It is not easy for him to be alone in the United States.

8. Building family ties in the United States is very important for all of us. My brother ███ would love to stay forever in the United States because he loves his country, the United States and the good opportunities, medical benefits and protection he has there compared to living here in the Philippines, where medical help and assistance is difficult and very expensive. My brother Jose has never been selfish to his loved ones. He loved our mother unconditionally. I get emotionally stressed and suffer from mental / emotional hardship when he needs help or gets ill but nobody is there to take care of him. I feel very sorry and guilty that I cannot be there with him during the moment of an emergency. All of us are still suffering from hardship due to the unexpected death of our beloved mother, reuniting in the United States will help us heal the pain and sorrow that we are all currently experiencing.

9. Family is very important for me and I want to help and support my brother and take care of him to make sure that he will be safe and have someone to depend on when any medical or emergency needs arise.

10. My brother ███ is residing alone in the United States for past 4 years, since our mother died. He is suffering a life threatening illness and is currently being seen and monitored regularly by a Kaiser Specialist doctor Darvin Scott Smith MD and a Psychologist for his depression and anxiety. My brother has to take expensive specialty medications daily and for the rest of his life to prevent deterioration of his general health and to keep him alive. Currently my brother is not a burden to the state government; his health insurance pays for those medications. Jose is still able to function and work 40 hrs a week as Physical Therapist in the United States for the sake of his family living in the Philippines.

11. If my I-130 is not reinstated, my brother ███ will need to return to the Philippines because he is alone in the United States and cannot survive there alone. If he comes to the Philippines, I do not believe there are adequate health facilities in the Philippines for him. The doctors and hospitals in the United States are aware of his conditions. They can easily access the records of what was prescribed. If he was in the Philippines, this could not occur. I pray that my brother will stay healthy but I also am aware that there is a possibility that he may get an illness or disease that will require medical attention. My brother's doctors are in the United States and would know the best way to treat him. If something goes wrong if he is in the Philippines, I am afraid he may not be able to stay as healthy as he would in the United States. From what I have seen and what I have been told, the medical care is better in the United States. I have sufficient reasons to believe that there aren't enough medical resources in the Philippines that he could receive. My brother is residing for past 16 years in the United States, will always be looked upon as an outsider in the Philippines. Even if he is a deserving candidate for a job, preference will be given to local people.

12. If I am not allowed to come to the United States, then my brother will face financial hardships as he will have to continue to provide us. The Philippines has a high rate of unemployment; it will be extremely difficult for us to survive in the Philippines. Poverty has been a persistent problem in the Philippines. Lack of and unavailability of education and unemployment are the major reasons for poverty in the Philippines. Life without a stable and well-paying job in the Philippines would be extremely difficult for us. The Philippines does not promote equal opportunity for employment.

13. I also worry about the growing violence in the Philippines. I fear for the safety of my brother. I am afraid that he can be victim of violent crimes, such as kidnapping, carjacking, and robbery by organized criminal groups. I also fear that because my brother is an American, he will be easily targeted to gangs because they will think he has money. The economy in the Philippines is very poor and it will be very difficult to live in the Philippines knowing how the situation is. There are numerous problems in the Philippines like high crime rates, drugs, corruption, and a troubled economy. He is accustomed with the American Culture and living in the Philippines will be a mental burden to him. America is a land of opportunities unlike the Philippines.

14. If my mother's I -130 petition is not reinstated, then my brother ███ will need to file a new I-130 and I will need to wait for another 23 years for a visa number to become current.

15. Please give me opportunity to let my family stay together. We all love each other and promise that we will continue to be a loving family and productive members to society, if you allow our family to stay intact. I beg you from the bottom of my heart, to consider this application and reinstate my Form I -130.

16. I am waiting for more than 8 years for my mother's petition to be current and that I should not be penalized for my mother's death.

17. I declare under penalty of perjury pursuant to the law of the United States that the foregoing is true and correct.

Date: September 14, 2017 Declarant: ████████

Exhibit 2:

Declaration of Beneficiary's U.S. Citizen Brother

I, [REDACTED] hereby declare as follows:

1. I have personal knowledge of all the facts contained in this declaration, and if called upon to testify I would do so.

2. I reside at [REDACTED] USA.

3. I was born on August 6, 1971in Manila, Philippines. I became a U.S. citizen on August 22, 2006 through Naturalization. I have two brothers; 51-year-old [REDACTED] and 50-year-old [REDACTED] and two sisters; 53-year-old [REDACTED] nd 48-year-old [REDACTED] All my brothers and sisters are citizens of the Philippines.

4. On December 18, 2008, my U.S. citizen mother, [REDACTED] filed an I-130 pursuant to INA § 203(a)(2)(B) for which the beneficiary was my brother, [REDACTED] which was approved on November 19, 2009. Unfortunately, my mother died on June 28, 2013.

5. I have been living here in the United States for almost 16 years now but since my mother's untimely death on June 28, 2013; I have been suffering from hardship being alone. My brother and sister too are experiencing hardship about her death. I don't have any family members or any relatives who live here in the United States. I am the only one who lives here now.

6. The impact of the revocation of the I-130 for my brother [REDACTED] will definitely cause extreme hardship for me as a U.S. citizen. I am suffering from HIV/Aids infection, history of Hepatitis C, Gastro-Oesophageal Reflux disease, Testicular failure with hypogonadism, insomnia, and major depressive disorder recurrent episode and I am currently being seen and monitored regularly by a Kaiser Specialist doctor Darvin Scott Smith MD and a Psychologist for my depression and anxiety. I have to take expensive specialty medications daily and for the rest of my life. To prevent deterioration of my general health and to keep me alive. Currently I am not a burden to the state government; my health insurance pays for those medications. I am residing alone in the United States and due to death of my mother I am suffering from emotional depression. I can still able to work 40 hours a week as a physical therapist for the sake of family living in the Philippines. I have no choice but to stay alive for them because I love them. I am trying my best to stay emotionally strong for them but I have to admit it's a daily mental and

emotional challenge for me to have a stable mental health and I don't know if I can cope and for how long I don't know. My mental health is not as good as before because of the things that happened in my life and I do worry a lot about my future and my life in general and my family in the Philippines I love my family, I will do everything for them. When I am not feeling well sometimes I push myself to go to work because I have to. I am filing a form I-864 as a substitute sponsor for my brother and I am only the qualified relative for the same.

7. I desperately need my older brother and sister to come here and live here for emotional and psychological support because for me it's very important. I don't have anybody who can help me here that I can trust. My loved ones are the only people who can help me cope with stresses and depression in my life. I don't know what will be my health condition in the coming years. I need my family on my side for support and to help me when I need help just in case of any emergency.

8. The hardship is not only to me but also to my brother ■■■■ They will be worried for me if I get sick and I am hoping not. They want to be here to take care of their younger brother when that time comes. I cannot reunite to live with them in the Philippines; I have to live here in the United States for good because of the medical care that I will always need, that can be paid by my health insurance. The medical care in the Philippines is not good compared here in the States. Reuniting with them living there for long time is not possible, because I need to get my medications and see my specialist doctors on a regular basis. The only best way is for them to live with me. I want them to live here so that they can help me cope with my depression and physical illness. I don't want to be always sad and feel unsafe, I don't want to be a burden to any other people I don't know. I want my older brother and sister to be here with me for my mind to be at peace. I don't want to be sad anymore. I want to reunite with them here. I will feel safer and secure if they are here.

9. Emotional hardships are the most difficult thing that I and my older brother and sister will be dealing forever in case their I-130 is not reinstated. I have been taking care and supporting them for many years, I hope immigration will reinstate their I-130 to give them the chance to take care of me just in case when the need arise. I have to honestly admit that I will be more scared of my future and my depression and illness might get worse if they will never be given the chance to come here. It's hard for me living alone without them. Hope you understand my condition. I am speaking through my heart, I am hoping for them to be able to reunite with me here and definitely it will make me happy and feel secure and not to worry anymore. My older brother and sister are nice people, I know that they want to come here to return the favor and take care of their younger brother. We have a very close family, we help each other; please don't deprive us to

reunite here in the States. I hope for your mercy, humanitarian kindness and understanding.

10. If their I-130 is not reinstated then I may need to move to the Philippines and If I move, I will face extreme hardships.

11. I do not believe there are adequate health facilities in the Philippines for me. My doctors and hospitals are aware of my conditions. They can easily access the records of what has been prescribed. If I was in the Philippines, this could not occur. I pray that I will stay healthy, but I also am aware that there is a possibility that I may get an illness or disease that will require medical attention. My doctors are here and would know the best way to treat me. If something goes wrong if I was in the Philippines, I am afraid I may not be able to stay as healthy as I will here. From what I have seen and what I have been told, the medical care is better in the United States. I have sufficient reasons to believe that there aren't enough medical resources in the Philippines that I should be receiving. Even if there were any medical resources, it would be impossible for me to obtain them. Medicine in the Philippines is very expensive.

12. I also worry about the growing violence in the Philippines. I fear for the safety of myself. I am afraid that we can be victims of violent crimes, such as kidnapping, carjacking, and robbery by organized criminal groups. I also fear that because I am an American, I will be easy target to gangs because they will think I have money. The economy in the Philippines is very poor and it will be very difficult to live in Philippines knowing how the situation is. There are numerous problems in Philippines like high crime rates, drugs, corruption, and a troubled economy. I am accustomed with the American Culture and living in the Philippines will be a mental burden to me. America is a land of opportunities unlike the Philippines.

13. For the foregoing reasons, please reinstate my brother's I-130, so that my brother can immigrate to United States soon.

14. I declare under penalty of perjury pursuant to the law of the State of California that the foregoing is true and correct.

Date: SEPTEMBER 7, 2017 Declarant: ____________

Exhibit 3:

Copy of Beneficiary's Certificate of Birth

Page 1 of 1, 2 Copies

Municipal Form No. 102 - (Revised Dec. 1, 1930)

(TO BE ACCOMPLISHED IN DUPLICATE)

REPUBLIC OF THE PHILIPPINES

CERTIFICATE OF LIVE BIRTH

(FILL OUT COMPLETELY, ACCURATELY, LEGIBLY IN INK OR TYPEWRITER)

Province:

City or Municipality: MANILA

Register Number:
(a) Civil Registrar-General No.
(b) Local Civil Registrar No. 1073 (1966)

1. Place of Birth
a. Province
b. City or Municipality MANILA
c. Name of Hospital or Institution: MATERNITY AND CHILDREN'S HOSPITAL
d. Is Place of Birth Inside City Limits? Yes x No

2. Usual Residence of Mother (Where does mother live?)
a. Province
b. City or Municipality MANILA
c. Number and Street 1953 Muñoz
d. Is Residence Inside City Limits? Yes x No
e. Is Residence on a Farm? Yes No x

CHILD
3. Name (Type or print) First Middle Last
4. Sex MALE
5a. This Birth Single x Twin Triplet
5b. If twin or triplet, was child 1st 2nd 3rd
6. Date of Birth Month Feb. Day 10 Year 1966

FATHER
7. Name First Jose Middle Villaflor Last Capistrano
Religion Cath.
8. Nationality Fil.
8a. Race Brown
9. Age (At time of this birth) Years 38
10. Birthplace Serema, Cam. Sur
11a. Usual Occupation Govt. Employee
11b. Kind of Business or Industry

MOTHER
12. Maiden Name First Lourdes Middle Aranilla Last Paner
Religion Cath.
13. Nationality Fil.
13a. Race Brown
14. Age (At time of this birth) Years 33
15. Birthplace Manila
16. Previous Deliveries to Mother (Do not include this birth)
a. How many children are now living? 1
b. How many other children were born alive but are now dead? 0
c. How many fetal deaths (fetuses born dead any time after conception)? 0

17a. Informant's Signature *Lourdes P. Capistrano*
b. Name in Print
c. Address

18. Mother's Mailing Address (Number, Street, City or Municipality, Province)
1953 Muñoz, Paco, Manila

19. ATTENDANT AT BIRTH
I hereby certify that I attended the birth of this child who was born alive at 11:45 o'clock A.M. on the date above indicated.
c. Signature: [signature]
b. Name in Print: L. D. ... SARINGEN
d. Date Signed by Attendant at Birth: 3/1/66
e. Title of Attendant at Birth: M.D. x Nurse Midwife Others (Specify)

20. Received in the Office of the Local Civil Registrar by:
a. Signature:
b. Name in Print:
c. Title or Position:
d. Date: MAR 3 1966

21. a. Given Name Added from Supplemental Report:
b. Date When Given Name was Supplied: 0390

22a. Length of Pregnancy 40 Completed Weeks
22b. Weight at Birth ... lbs. 15 ozs.
23. Legitimate Yes x No

24. Date and Place of Marriage of Parents (For legitimate birth)
May (Month) 22 (Day), 1963 (Year)
City or Municipality MANILA, Province

25. This Certificate is Prepared by:
Signature: *A. Estrella*
Name in Print: A. Estrella
Title or Position: CLERK
Date: Feb. 19, 1966

(SPACE FOR MEDICAL AND HEALTH USE FOR SPECIAL PURPOSES)

RESERVE FOR BINDING

04961-H4-144EBP-00282-BI001

BEST POSSIBLE IMAGE

BReN
03900-A66CK30-5

Documentary
Stamp Tax Paid

[signature]
CARMELITA N. ERICTA
Administrator and Civil Registrar General
National Statistics Office

Exhibit 4:

Copy of Petitioner's Certificate of Death

STATE OF CALIFORNIA

CERTIFICATION OF VITAL RECORD

COUNTY of SANTA CLARA

PUBLIC HEALTH DEPARTMENT

VITAL RECORDS AND REGISTRATION

CERTIFICATE OF DEATH 3201343005421

P

02/11/1933 80 F

PHILIPPINES [X] NO WIDOWED 08/28/2013 1216

BACHELOR [X] NO FILIPINO

TEACHER ELEMENTARY EDUCATION 20

338 SOUTH FREMONT STREET

SAN MATEO SAN MATEO 94401 6 CALIFORNIA

JOSE CAPISTRANO, SON 338 SOUTH FREMONT STREET, SAN MATEO, CA 94401

JOSE V. PI

PI

07/14/2013 MANILA MEMORIAL DASMARINAS, CAVITE CITY, PHILIPPINES

TR/BU DAVID FECHTER EMB7075

DUGGANS SERRA MORTUARY FD1096 MARTIN D FENSTERSHEIB, MD 07/08/2013

STANFORD MEDICAL CENTER [X] IP

SANTA CLARA 300 PASTEUR DRIVE STANFORD

COMPLICATIONS OF LEFT HIP FRACTURE DAYS [X] YES 13-02388

[X] NO

[X] YES

[X] YES

LEFT LUNG LOBAR PNEUMONIA; ATHEROSCLEROTIC CARDIOVASCULAR DISEASE; SYSTEMIC HYPERTENSION

LEFT HIP CEMENTED ARTHROPLASTY 08/08/2013 [X] NO

[X] Accident [X] NO 08/22/2013 1000

OWN RESIDENCE

FOUND TO HAVE FALLEN WHILE WALKING TO BATHROOM

338 SOUTH FREMONT STREET #117, SAN MATEO, CA 94401

JOSEPH PATRICK O'HARA 07/08/2013 JOSEPH PATRICK O'HARA, MD

CERTIFIED COPY OF VITAL RECORDS

STATE OF CALIFORNIA, COUNTY OF SANTA CLARA } SS. DATE ISSUED JUL 10 2013

H2499669

This is a true and exact reproduction of the document officially registered and placed on file in the VITAL RECORDS SECTION, DEPARTMENT OF PUBLIC HEALTH.

MARTIN D. FENSTERSHEIB, HEALTH OFFICER AND LOCAL REGISTRAR OF BIRTHS AND DEATHS

This copy not valid unless prepared on engraved border displaying seal and signature of Registrar.

Exhibit 5:

Copy of Approval Notice of Form I-130 of Beneficiary

Department of Homeland Security
U.S. Citizenship and Immigration Services

I-797, Notice of Action

THE UNITED STATES OF AMERICA

RECEIPT NUMBER		CASE TYPE
WAC-09-076-14030		I130 IMMIGRANT PETITION FOR RELATIVE, FIANCE(E), OR ORPHAN
RECEIPT DATE	PRIORITY DATE	PETITIONER
December 18, 2008	December 14, 2008	[redacted]
NOTICE DATE	PAGE	BENEFICIARY
November 19, 2009	1 of 1	[redacted]

Notice Type: Approval Notice
Section: Unmarried child 21/older of permanent resident, 203(a)(2)(B) INA

The above petition has been approved. We have sent the original visa petition to the Department of State National Visa Center (NVC), 32 Rochester Avenue, Portsmouth, NH 03801-2909. NVC processes all approved immigrant visa petitions that need consular action. It also determines which consular post is the appropriate consulate to complete visa processing. NVC will then forward the approved petition to that consulate.

The NVC will contact the person for whom you are petitioning (beneficiary) concerning further immigrant visa processing steps.

If you have any questions about visa issuance, please contact the NVC directly. However, please allow at least 90 days before calling the NVC if your beneficiary has not received correspondence from the NVC. The telephone number of the NVC is (603) 334-0700.

The approval of this visa petition does not in itself grant any immigration status and does not guarantee that the alien beneficiary will subsequently be found to be eligible for a visa, for admission to the United States, or for an extension, change, or adjustment of status.

THIS FORM IS NOT A VISA NOR MAY IT BE USED IN PLACE OF A VISA.

Please see the additional information on the back. You will be notified separately about any other cases you filed.
U.S. CITIZENSHIP & IMMIGRATION SVC
CALIFORNIA SERVICE CENTER
P. O. BOX 30111
LAGUNA NIGUEL CA 92607-0111
Customer Service Telephone: (800) 375-5283

Form I-797 (Rev. 01/31/05) N

Exhibit 6:

Copy of Naturalization Certificate of Beneficiary's U.S. Citizen Brother

THE UNITED STATES OF AMERICA

No. 29576341

CERTIFICATE OF NATURALIZATION

Personal description of holder as of date of naturalization:

Date of birth: AUGUST 06, 1971

Sex: MALE

Height: 5 feet inches

Marital status: SINGLE

Country of former nationality: PHILIPPINES

CIS Registration No: [redacted]

I certify that the description given is true, and that the photograph affixed hereto is a likeness of me.

Be it known that, pursuant to an application filed with the Secretary of Homeland Security

at: SAN FRANCISCO, CALIFORNIA

The Secretary having found that:

then residing in the United States, intends to reside in the United States when so required by the Naturalization Laws of the United States, and had in all other respects complied with the applicable provisions of such naturalization laws and was entitled to be admitted to citizenship, such person having taken the oath of allegiance in a ceremony conducted by the

US CITIZENSHIP AND IMMIGRATION SERVICES

at: SAN FRANCISCO, CALIFORNIA on: AUGUST 22, 2006

that such person is admitted as a citizen of the United States of America.

IT IS PUNISHABLE BY U. S. LAW TO COPY, PRINT OR PHOTOGRAPH THIS CERTIFICATE, WITHOUT LAWFUL AUTHORITY.

Director, U. S. Citizenship and Immigration Services

DEPARTMENT OF HOMELAND SECURITY

Exhibit 7:

Copy of Tax Returns of Beneficiary's U.S. Citizen Brother for Years 2013-2016

FILE COPY

2016
Income Tax Return

Prepared For:

Prepared By:

et

Form 1040 Department of the Treasury—Internal Revenue Service **U.S. Individual Income Tax Return 2016** OMB No. 1545-0074 **FILE COPY**

See separate instructions.

Your social security number: 318-94-4769

Spouse's social security number

Make sure the SSN(s) above and on line 6c are correct.

Presidential Election Campaign — You / Spouse

Filing Status

1 [X] Single
2 [ ] Married filing jointly (even if only one had income)
3 [ ] Married filing separately. Enter spouse's SSN above and full name here. ▶
4 [ ] Head of household (with qualifying person). (See instructions.) If the qualifying person is a child but not your dependent, enter this child's name here. ▶
5 [ ] Qualifying widow(er) with dependent child

Check only one box.

Exemptions

6a [X] Yourself. If someone can claim you as a dependent, do not check box 6a
b [ ] Spouse

c Dependents: (1) First name, Last name; (2) Dependent's social security number; (3) Dependent's relationship to you; (4) ✓ if child under age 17 qualifying for child tax credit

If more than four dependents, see instructions and check here ▶ [ ]

d Total number of exemptions claimed

Boxes checked on 6a and 6b	1
No. of children on 6c who: • lived with you	0
• did not live with you due to divorce or separation (see instructions)	0
Dependents on 6c not entered above	0
Add numbers on lines above ▶	1

Income

Attach Form(s) W-2 here. Also attach Forms W-2G and 1099-R if tax was withheld.

If you did not get a W-2, see instructions.

7	Wages, salaries, tips, etc. Attach Form(s) W-2	7	50.
8a	Taxable interest. Attach Schedule B if required	8a	
b	Tax-exempt interest. Do not include on line 8a — 8b		
9a	Ordinary dividends. Attach Schedule B if required	9a	
b	Qualified dividends — 9b		
10	Taxable refunds, credits, or offsets of state and local income taxes	10	
11	Alimony received	11	
12	Business income or (loss). Attach Schedule C or C-EZ	12	74,388.
13	Capital gain or (loss). Attach Schedule D if required. If not required, check here ▶ [ ]	13	
14	Other gains or (losses). Attach Form 4797	14	
15a	IRA distributions — 15a; b Taxable amount	15b	
16a	Pensions and annuities — 16a; b Taxable amount	16b	
17	Rental real estate, royalties, partnerships, S corporations, trusts, etc. Attach Schedule E	17	
18	Farm income or (loss). Attach Schedule F	18	
19	Unemployment compensation	19	
20a	Social security benefits — 20a; b Taxable amount	20b	
21	Other income. List type and amount	21	
22	Combine the amounts in the far right column for lines 7 through 21. This is your total income ▶	22	74,438.

Adjusted Gross Income

23	Educator expenses	23			
24	Certain business expenses of reservists, performing artists, and fee-basis government officials. Attach Form 2106 or 2106-EZ	24			
25	Health savings account deduction. Attach Form 8889	25			
26	Moving expenses. Attach Form 3903	26			
27	Deductible part of self-employment tax. Attach Schedule SE	27	5,256.		
28	Self-employed SEP, SIMPLE, and qualified plans	28			
29	Self-employed health insurance deduction	29	14,400.		
30	Penalty on early withdrawal of savings	30			
31a	Alimony paid b Recipient's SSN ▶	31a			
32	IRA deduction	32			
33	Student loan interest deduction	33			
34	Tuition and fees. Attach Form 8917	34			
35	Domestic production activities deduction. Attach Form 8903	35			
36	Add lines 23 through 35			36	19,656.
37	Subtract line 36 from line 22. This is your adjusted gross income ▶			37	54,782.

For Disclosure, Privacy Act, and Paperwork Reduction Act Notice, see separate instructions. Form 1040 (2016)

Form 1040 (2016) Page 2

Section	Line	Description		Amount	Line	Amount
Tax and Credits	38	Amount from line 37 (adjusted gross income)			38	54,782.
	39a	Check if: ☐ You were born before January 2, 1952, ☐ Blind. ☐ Spouse was born before January 2, 1952, ☐ Blind. Total boxes checked ▶ 39a		0		
	b	If your spouse itemizes on a separate return or you were a dual-status alien, check here ▶ 39b ☐				
Standard Deduction for–	40	Itemized deductions (from Schedule A) or your standard deduction (see left margin)			40	6,300.
	41	Subtract line 40 from line 38			41	48,482.
	42	Exemptions. If line 38 is $155,650 or less, multiply $4,050 by the number on line 6d. Otherwise, see instructions			42	4,050.
	43	Taxable income. Subtract line 42 from line 41. If line 42 is more than line 41, enter -0-			43	44,432.
	44	Tax (see instructions). Check if any from: a ☐ Form(s) 8814 b ☐ Form 4972 c ☐			44	6,878.
	45	Alternative minimum tax (see instructions). Attach Form 6251			45	
	46	Excess advance premium tax credit repayment. Attach Form 8962			46	
	47	Add lines 44, 45, and 46 ▶			47	6,878.
	48	Foreign tax credit. Attach Form 1116 if required	48			
	49	Credit for child and dependent care expenses. Attach Form 2441	49			
	50	Education credits from Form 8863, line 19	50			
	51	Retirement savings contributions credit. Attach Form 8880	51			
	52	Child tax credit. Attach Schedule 8812, if required	52			
	53	Residential energy credits. Attach Form 5695	53			
	54	Other credits from Form: a ☐ 3800 b ☐ 8801 c ☐	54			
	55	Add lines 48 through 54. These are your total credits			55	0.
	56	Subtract line 55 from line 47. If line 55 is more than line 47, enter -0- ▶			56	6,878.
Other Taxes	57	Self-employment tax. Attach Schedule SE			57	10,511.
	58	Unreported social security and Medicare tax from Form: a ☐ 4137 b ☐ 8919			58	
	59	Additional tax on IRAs, other qualified retirement plans, etc. Attach Form 5329 if required			59	
	60a	Household employment taxes from Schedule H			60a	
	b	First-time homebuyer credit repayment. Attach Form 5405 if required			60b	
	61	Health care: individual responsibility (see instructions) Full-year coverage ☐			61	
	62	Taxes from: a ☐ Form 8959 b ☐ Form 8960 c ☐ Instructions; enter code(s)			62	
	63	Add lines 56 through 62. This is your total tax ▶			63	17,389.
Payments	64	Federal income tax withheld from Forms W-2 and 1099	64	1.		
	65	2016 estimated tax payments and amount applied from 2015 return	65			
If you have a qualifying child, attach Schedule EIC.	66a	Earned income credit (EIC) NO	66a			
	b	Nontaxable combat pay election 66b				
	67	Additional child tax credit. Attach Schedule 8812	67			
	68	American opportunity credit from Form 8863, line 8	68			
	69	Net premium tax credit. Attach Form 8962	69			
	70	Amount paid with request for extension to file	70			
	71	Excess social security and tier 1 RRTA tax withheld	71			
	72	Credit for federal tax on fuels. Attach Form 4136	72			
	73	Credits from Form: a ☐ 2439 b ☒ Reserved c ☐ 8885 d ☐	73			
	74	Add lines 64, 65, 66a, and 67 through 73. These are your total payments ▶			74	1.
Refund	75	If line 74 is more than line 63, subtract line 63 from line 74. This is the amount you overpaid			75	0.
	76a	Amount of line 75 you want refunded to you. If Form 8888 is attached, check here ▶ ☐			76a	0.
Direct deposit? See instructions.	▶ b	Routing number ▶ c Type: ☐ Checking ☐ Savings				
	▶ d	Account number				
	77	Amount of line 75 you want applied to your 2017 estimated tax ▶	77			
Amount You Owe	78	Amount you owe. Subtract line 74 from line 63. For details on how to pay, see instructions ▶			78	17,774.
	79	Estimated tax penalty (see instructions)	79	386.		

Third Party Designee Do you want to allow another person to discuss this return with the IRS (see instructions)? ☐ Yes. Complete below. ☒ No
Designee's name ▶ Phone no. ▶ Personal identification number (PIN) ▶

Sign Here
Joint return? See instructions. Keep a copy for your records.
Your signature | Date | Your occupation: Home Health Care PT | Daytime phone number: (650)515-1208
Spouse's signature. If a joint return, both must sign. | Date | Spouse's occupation | If the IRS sent you an Identity Protection PIN, enter it here (see inst.)

Paid Preparer Use Only
Print/Type preparer's name: Lucina V de los Reyes | Preparer's signature | Date: 9/1/17 | Check ☒ if self-employed | PTIN: P01204841
Firm's name ▶ Lucina V de los Reyes | Firm's EIN ▶ 27-2432384
Firm's address ▶ 1529 Hampton Court, Naperville, IL 60565 | Phone no. (630)983-6227

www.irs.gov/form1040 Form 1040 (2016)

SCHEDULE C (Form 1040)

Department of the Treasury Internal Revenue Service (99)

Profit or Loss From Business

(Sole Proprietorship)

▶ Information about Schedule C and its separate instructions is at www.irs.gov/schedulec.

▶ Attach to Form 1040, 1040NR, or 1041; partnerships generally must file Form 1065.

OMB No. 1545-0074

2016

Attachment Sequence No. 09

Name of proprietor: ████ | Social security number (SSN): ████

A Principal business or profession, including product or service (see instructions): Travelling Physical Therapist

B Enter code from instructions ▶ ████

C Business name. If no separate business name, leave blank.

D Employer ID number (EIN) (see instr.)

E Business address (including suite or room no.) ▶

City, town or post office, state, and ZIP code

F Accounting method: (1) ☒ Cash (2) ☐ Accrual (3) ☐ Other (specify) ▶

G Did you "materially participate" in the operation of this business during 2016? If "No," see instructions for limit on losses ☒ Yes ☐ No

H If you started or acquired this business during 2016, check here ▶ ☐

I Did you make any payments in 2016 that would require you to file Form(s) 1099? (see instructions) ☐ Yes ☐ No

J If "Yes," did you or will you file required Forms 1099? ☐ Yes ☐ No

Part I Income

1	Gross receipts or sales. See instructions for line 1 and check the box if this income was reported to you on Form W-2 and the "Statutory employee" box on that form was checked ▶ ☐	1	192,388.
2	Returns and allowances	2	
3	Subtract line 2 from line 1	3	192,388.
4	Cost of goods sold (from line 42)	4	
5	**Gross profit.** Subtract line 4 from line 3	5	192,388.
6	Other income, including federal and state gasoline or fuel tax credit or refund (see instructions)	6	
7	**Gross income.** Add lines 5 and 6 ▶	7	192,388.

Part II Expenses. Enter expenses for business use of your home **only** on line 30.

		Line	Amount			Line	Amount
8	Advertising	8		18	Office expense (see instructions)	18	
9	Car and truck expenses (see instructions)	9	40,500.	19	Pension and profit-sharing plans	19	
				20	Rent or lease (see instructions):		
10	Commissions and fees	10			a Vehicles, machinery, and equipment	20a	
11	Contract labor (see instructions)	11			b Other business property	20b	
12	Depletion	12		21	Repairs and maintenance	21	
13	Depreciation and section 179 expense deduction (not included in Part III) (see instructions)	13		22	Supplies (not included in Part III)	22	3,000.
				23	Taxes and licenses	23	
				24	Travel, meals, and entertainment:		
14	Employee benefit programs (other than on line 19)	14			a Travel	24a	27,000.
15	Insurance (other than health)	15	2,500.		b Deductible meals and entertainment (see instructions)	24b	
16	Interest:			25	Utilities	25	
	a Mortgage (paid to banks, etc.)	16a		26	Wages (less employment credits)	26	
	b Other	16b		27a	Other expenses (from line 48)	27a	9,700.
17	Legal and professional services	17	35,300.		b Reserved for future use	27b	

28	**Total expenses** before expenses for business use of home. Add lines 8 through 27a ▶	28	118,000.
29	Tentative profit or (loss). Subtract line 28 from line 7	29	74,388.
30	Expenses for business use of your home. Do not report these expenses elsewhere. Attach Form 8829 unless using the simplified method (see instructions). **Simplified method filers only:** enter the total square footage of: (a) your home ____ and (b) the part of your home used for business: ____. Use the Simplified Method Worksheet in the instructions to figure the amount to enter on line 30	30	
31	**Net profit or (loss).** Subtract line 30 from line 29. • If a profit, enter on both **Form 1040, line 12** (or **Form 1040NR, line 13**) and on **Schedule SE, line 2.** (If you checked the box on line 1, see instructions). Estates and trusts, enter on **Form 1041, line 3.** • If a loss, you **must** go to line 32.	31	74,388.

32 If you have a loss, check the box that describes your investment in this activity (see instructions).

• If you checked 32a, enter the loss on both **Form 1040, line 12,** (or **Form 1040NR, line 13**) and on **Schedule SE, line 2.** (If you checked the box on line 1, see the line 31 instructions). Estates and trusts, enter on **Form 1041, line 3.**

• If you checked 32b, you **must** attach **Form 6198.** Your loss may be limited.

32a ☐ All investment is at risk.

32b ☐ Some investment is not at risk.

For Paperwork Reduction Act Notice, see the separate instructions. Schedule C (Form 1040) 2016

LHA 09/11/2017 09:10:24

Schedule C (Form 1040) 2016 Page 2

Part III **Cost of Goods Sold** (see instructions)

33 Method(s) used to value closing inventory: a ☐ Cost b ☐ Lower of cost or market c ☐ Other (attach explanation)

34 Was there any change in determining quantities, costs, or valuations between opening and closing inventory? If "Yes," attach explanation ☐ Yes ☐ No

35 Inventory at beginning of year. If different from last year's closing inventory, attach explanation	35	
36 Purchases less cost of items withdrawn for personal use	36	
37 Cost of labor. Do not include any amounts paid to yourself	37	
38 Materials and supplies	38	
39 Other costs	39	
40 Add lines 35 through 39	40	
41 Inventory at end of year	41	
42 Cost of goods sold. Subtract line 41 from line 40. Enter the result here and on line 4	42	0.

Part IV **Information on Your Vehicle.** Complete this part **only** if you are claiming car or truck expenses on line 9 and are not required to file Form 4562 for this business. See the instructions for line 13 to find out if you must file Form 4562.

43 When did you place your vehicle in service for business purposes? (month, day, year) ▶ 02/25/2002

44 Of the total number of miles you drove your vehicle during 2016, enter the number of miles you used your vehicle for:

a Business 75000 b Commuting (see instructions) 0. c Other 0

45 Was your vehicle available for personal use during off-duty hours? ☒ Yes ☐ No

46 Do you (or your spouse) have another vehicle available for personal use? ☒ Yes ☐ No

47a Do you have evidence to support your deduction? ☐ Yes ☐ No

b If "Yes," is the evidence written? ☐ Yes ☐ No

Part V **Other Expenses.** List below business expenses not included on lines 8–26 or line 30.

Uniform/upkeep	2,000.
Cellphone, Phone bills	2,500.
Internet	1,500.
PT tools	2,500.
Car registration	700.
Parking fees/tolls	500.
48 Total other expenses. Enter here and on line 27a 48	9,700.

Schedule C (Form 1040) 2016

SCHEDULE SE (Form 1040)

Department of the Treasury Internal Revenue Service (99)

Self-Employment Tax

▶ Information about Schedule SE and its separate instructions is at *www.irs.gov/schedulese*.

▶ Attach to Form 1040 or Form 1040NR.

OMB No. 1545-0074

2016

Attachment Sequence No. **17**

Name of person with **self-employment** income (as shown on Form 1040 or Form 1040NR)	Social security number of person with self-employment income ▶
[redacted]	[redacted]

Before you begin: To determine if you must file Schedule SE, see the instructions.

May I Use Short Schedule SE or Must I Use Long Schedule SE?

Note. Use this flowchart **only** if you must file Schedule SE. If unsure, see *Who Must File Schedule SE* in the instructions.

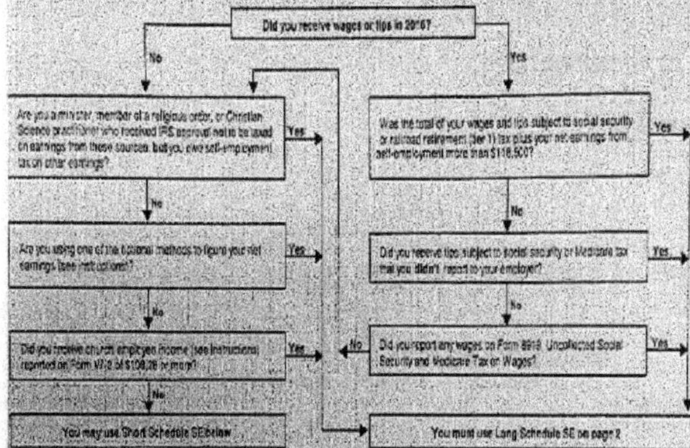

Section A—Short Schedule SE. Caution. Read above to see if you can use Short Schedule SE.

1a Net farm profit or (loss) from Schedule F, line 34, and farm partnerships, Schedule K-1 (Form 1065), box 14, code A	1a	
b If you received social security retirement or disability benefits, enter the amount of Conservation Reserve Program payments included on Schedule F, line 4b, or listed on Schedule K-1 (Form 1065), box 20, code Z	1b	( )
2 Net profit or (loss) from Schedule C, line 31; Schedule C-EZ, line 3; Schedule K-1 (Form 1065), box 14, code A (other than farming); and Schedule K-1 (Form 1065-B), box 9, code J1. Ministers and members of religious orders, see instructions for types of income to report on this line. See instructions for other income to report	2	74,388.
3 Combine lines 1a, 1b, and 2	3	74,388.
4 Multiply line 3 by 92.35% (0.9235). If less than $400, you don't owe self-employment tax; **don't** file this schedule unless you have an amount on line 1b ▶	4	68,697.
Note. If line 4 is less than $400 due to Conservation Reserve Program payments on line 1b, see instructions.		
5 **Self-employment tax.** If the amount on line 4 is: • $118,500 or less, multiply line 4 by 15.3% (0.153). Enter the result here and on **Form 1040, line 57,** or **Form 1040NR, line 55** • More than $118,500, multiply line 4 by 2.9% (0.029). Then, add $14,694 to the result. Enter the total here and on **Form 1040, line 57,** or **Form 1040NR, line 55**	5	10,511.
6 **Deduction for one-half of self-employment tax.** Multiply line 5 by 50% (0.50). Enter the result here and on **Form 1040, line 27,** or **Form 1040NR, line 27** — 6 — 5,256.		

For Paperwork Reduction Act Notice, see your tax return instructions. Schedule SE (Form 1040) 2016

☐ CORRECTED (if checked)

PAYER'S name, street address, city or town, state or province, country, ZIP or foreign postal code, and telephone no.	1 Rents	OMB No. 1545-0115	Miscellaneous Income
AMITY HOME HEALTH CARE 21029465 INC (510)289-1250 27171 CALAROGO AVE STE 100 HAYWARD CA 94545	$ 2 Royalties $	2016 Form 1099-MISC	
	3 Other income $	4 Federal income tax withheld $	Copy 2
PAYER'S federal identification number: 45-2123003 / RECIPIENT'S identification number:	5 Fishing boat proceeds $	6 Medical and health care payments $	To be filed with recipient's state income tax return, when required.
RECIPIENT'S name Street address (including apt. no.)	7 Nonemployee compensation $ 100987.00	8 Substitute payments in lieu of dividends or interest $	
City or town, state or province, country, and ZIP or foreign postal code	9 Payer made direct sales of $5,000 or more of consumer products to a buyer (recipient) for resale ► ☐	10 Crop insurance proceeds $	
	11	12	
Account number (see instructions) / FATCA filing requirement ☐	13 Excess golden parachute payments $	14 Gross proceeds paid to an attorney $	
15a Section 409A deferrals $ / 15b Section 409A income $	16 State tax withheld $ $	17 State/Payer's state no. CA004-9179 5	18 State income $ 100987.00 $

Form 1099-MISC www.irs.gov/form1099misc Department of the Treasury - Internal Revenue Service

☐ CORRECTED (if checked)

PAYER'S name, street address, city or town, state or province, country, ZIP or foreign postal code, and telephone no.		1 Rents	OMB No. 1545-0115	Miscellaneous Income
WARM SPRINGS HOME HEALTH, INC. 54 WHITNEY PLACE FREMONT, CA 94539 510-490-6988		$	2016	
		2 Royalties $	Form 1099-MISC	
		3 Other income $	4 Federal income tax withheld $	Copy B For Recipient
PAYER'S federal identification number 80-0084644	RECIPIENT'S identification number [redacted]	5 Fishing boat proceeds $	6 Medical and health care payments $	
RECIPIENT'S name, street address (including apt. no.), city or town, state or province, country, and ZIP or foreign postal code [redacted] [redacted] [redacted]		7 Nonemployee compensation $ 65997.50	8 Substitute payments in lieu of dividends or interest $	This is important tax information and is being furnished to the Internal Revenue Service. If you are required to file a return, a negligence penalty or other sanction may be imposed on you if this income is taxable and the IRS determines that it has not been reported.
		9 Payer made direct sales of $5,000 or more of consumer products to a buyer (recipient) for resale ▶ ☐	10 Crop insurance proceeds $	
		11	12	
Account number (see instructions)	FATCA filing requirement ☐	13 Excess golden parachute payments $	14 Gross proceeds paid to an attorney $	
15a Section 409A deferrals $	15b Section 409A income $	16 State tax withheld $ $	17 State/Payer's state no.	18 State income $ $

Form 1099-MISC (keep for your records) www.irs.gov/form1099misc Department of the Treasury - Internal Revenue Service

FORM #1 MISCREC

CALENDAR YEAR 2016 | 42 17001

MERIDIAN CARE INC
3900 NEWPARK MALL STE 209
NEWARK CA 94560

7 Nonemployee compensation $ 19328.00

Form 1099-MISC MISCELLANEOUS INCOME ☐ VOID ☐ CORRECTED COPY B, FOR RECIPIENT

CALENDAR YEAR	PAYER'S federal identification number	RECIPIENT'S identification number	Account number (see instructions)	
2016	20-5719568	318-94-4785	0942-A8808736 -	42 17001

PAYER'S name, street address, city or town, state or province, country, ZIP or foreign postal code, and telephone no.

MERIDIAN CARE INC
3900 NEWPARK MALL STE 209
NEWARK CA 94560

1 Rents	2 Royalties	3 Other income	4 Federal income tax withheld
$ 0.00	$ 0.00	$ 0.00	$
5 Fishing boat proceeds	6 Medical and health care payments	7 Nonemployee compensation	8 Substitute payments in lieu of dividends or interest
$	$	$ 19328.00	$
16 State tax withheld	17 State/Payer's state no.	18 State income	
$	CA/270-0030-6	$ 19328.00	

Form 1099-MISC MISCELLANEOUS INCOME ☐ VOID ☐ CORRECTED TO BE FILED WITH FEDERAL INCOME TAX RETURN IF NECESSARY

CALENDAR YEAR 2016 | 42 17001

MERIDIAN CARE INC
3900 NEWPARK MALL STE 209
NEWARK CA 94560

7 Nonemployee compensation $ 19328.00

☐ CORRECTED (if checked)

PAYER'S name, street address, city or town, state or province, country, ZIP or foreign postal code, and telephone no.		1 Rents	OMB No. 1545-0115	Miscellaneous Income
SOUTH SPRINGS HOME HEALTH CARE 1590 Oakland Rd B-213 San Jose, CA 95131 (408)883-4460		$ 2 Royalties $	2016 Form 1099-MISC	
		3 Other income $	4 Federal income tax withheld $	Copy B For Recipient
PAYER'S federal identification number [redacted]	RECIPIENT'S identification number [redacted]	5 Fishing boat proceeds $	6 Medical and health care payments $	
RECIPIENT'S name, street address (including apt. no.) city or town, state or province, country, and ZIP or foreign postal code [redacted]		7 Nonemployee compensation $ 5400.00	8 Substitute payments in lieu of dividends or interest $	This is important tax information and is being furnished to the Internal Revenue Service. If you are required to file a return, a negligence penalty or other sanction may be imposed on you if this income is taxable and the IRS determines that it has not been reported.
		9 Payer made direct sales of $5,000 or more of consumer products to a buyer (recipient) for resale ▶ ☐	10 Crop insurance proceeds $	
		11	12	
Account number (see instructions)	FATCA filing requirement ☐	13 Excess golden parachute payments $	14 Gross proceeds paid to an attorney $	
15a Section 409A deferrals $	15b Section 409A income $	16 State tax withheld $ $	17 State/Payer's state no.	18 State income $ $

Form **1099-MISC** (keep for your records) www.irs.gov/form1099misc Department of the Treasury - Internal Revenue Service

FILE COPY

FORM 540

2016 California Resident Income Tax Return

ATTACH FEDERAL RETURN

APE

[illegible]-94-4769 CAPI

16 PBA 62.610

JOSE CAPISTRANO

338 S FREMONT APT 117

SAN MATEO CA 94401

08-06-1971

1 [X] Single

2 [ ] Married/RDP filing jointly. See inst.

3 [ ] Married/RDP filing separately. Enter spouse's/RDP's SSN or ITIN above and full name here

If your California filing status is different from your federal filing status, check the box here [ ]

4 [ ] Head of household (with qualifying person). See instructions.

5 [ ] Qualifying widow(er) with dependent child. Enter year spouse/RDP died

6 If someone can claim you (or your spouse/RDP) as a dependent, check the box here. See instructions 6 [ ]

For line 7, line 8, line 9, and line 10: Multiply the amount you enter in the box by the pre-printed dollar amount for that line. Whole dollars only

7 Personal: If you checked box 1, 3, or 4 above, enter 1 in the box. If you checked box 2 or 5, enter 2 in the box. If you checked the box on line 6, see instructions. 7 [1] X $111 = $ 111.

8 Blind: If you (or your spouse/RDP) are visually impaired, enter 1; if both are visually impaired, enter 2. 8 [ ] X $111 = $

9 Senior: If you (or your spouse/RDP) are 65 or older, enter 1; if both are 65 or older, enter 2. 9 [ ] X $111 = $

10 Dependents: Do not include yourself or your spouse/RDP.

	Dependent 1	Dependent 2	Dependent 3
First name			
Last name			
SSN			
Dependent's relationship to you			

Total dependent exemptions 10 [ ] X $344 = $

11 Exemption amount: Add line 7 through line 10. Transfer this amount to line 32. 11 $ [illegible]

031 3101164

Form 540 C1 2016 Side 1

Your name: CAPISTRANO Your SSN or ITIN: 318-94-4769

Taxable Income

12	State wages from your Form(s) W-2, box 16	12	50.
13	Enter federal adjusted gross income from Form 1040, line 37; 1040A, line 21; or 1040EZ, line 4	13	54,782.
14	California adjustments - subtractions. Enter the amount from Schedule CA (540), line 37, column B	14	
15	Subtract line 14 from line 13. If less than zero, enter the result in parentheses. See instructions	15	54,782.
16	California adjustments - additions. Enter the amount from Schedule CA (540), line 37, column C	16	
17	California adjusted gross income. Combine line 15 and line 16	17	54,782.
18	Enter the larger of: Your California itemized deductions from Schedule CA (540), line 44; OR Your California standard deduction shown below for your filing status: • Single or Married/RDP filing separately . . . $4,129 • Married/RDP filing jointly, Head of household, or Qualifying widow(er) . . . $8,258. If Married/RDP filing separately or the box on line 6 is checked, STOP. See instructions	18	4,129.
19	Subtract line 18 from line 17. This is your taxable income. If less than zero, enter -0-	19	50,653.

Tax

31	Tax. Check box if from: [X] Tax Table [ ] Tax Rate Schedule [ ] FTB 3800 [ ] FTB 3803	31	2,163.
32	Exemption credits. Enter the amount from line 11. If your federal AGI is more than $182,459, see instr.	32	111.
33	Subtract line 32 from line 31. If less than zero, enter -0-	33	2,052.
34	Tax. See instructions. Check box if from: [ ] Schedule G-1 [ ] Form FTB 5870A	34	
35	Add line 33 and line 34	35	2,052.

Special Credits

40	Nonrefundable Child and Dependent Care Expenses Credit. See instructions	40	
43	Enter credit name ___ code ___ and amount	43	
44	Enter credit name ___ code ___ and amount	44	
45	To claim more than two credits, see instructions. Attach Schedule P (540)	45	
46	Nonrefundable renter's credit. See instructions	46	
47	Add line 40 through line 46. These are your total credits	47	0.
48	Subtract line 47 from line 35. If less than zero, enter -0-	48	2,052.

Other Taxes

61	Alternative minimum tax. Attach Schedule P (540)	61	
62	Mental Health Services Tax. See instructions	62	
63	Other taxes and credit recapture. See instructions	63	
64	Add line 48, line 61, line 62, and line 63. This is your total tax	64	2,052.

Side 2 Form 540 C1 2016 032 3122164

Your name [redacted] Your SSN or ITIN [redacted]

Payments

71	California income tax withheld. See instructions	• 71	
72	2016 CA estimated tax and other payments. See instructions	• 72	
73	Withholding (Form 592-B and/or 593). See instructions	• 73	
74	Excess SDI (or VPDI) withheld. See instructions	• 74	
75	Earned Income Tax Credit (EITC)	• 75	
76	Add lines 71 through 75. These are your total payments. See instructions	76	0.

Use Tax

91	Use Tax. See instructions	• 91	

Overpaid Tax/Tax Due

92	Payments balance. If line 76 is more than line 91, subtract line 91 from line 76	92	
93	Use Tax balance. If line 91 is more than line 76, subtract line 76 from line 91	93	
94	Overpaid tax. If line 92 is more than line 64, subtract line 64 from line 92	94	
95	Amount of line 94 you want applied to your 2017 estimated tax	• 95	
96	Overpaid tax available this year. Subtract line 95 from line 94	• 96	
97	Tax due. If line 92 is less than line 64, subtract line 92 from line 64	97	2,052.

031 3103164 Form 540 C1 2016

Your name [redacted] Your SSN or ITIN [redacted]

Contributions

	Code	Amount
California Seniors Special Fund. See instructions	• 400	
Alzheimer's Disease/Related Disorders Fund	• 401	
Rare and Endangered Species Preservation Program	• 403	
California Breast Cancer Research Fund	• 405	
California Firefighters' Memorial Fund	• 405	
Emergency Food for Families Fund	• 407	
California Peace Officer Memorial Foundation Fund	• 408	
California Sea Otter Fund	• 410	
California Cancer Research Fund	• 413	
Child Victims of Human Trafficking Fund	• 419	
School Supplies for Homeless Children Fund	• 422	
State Parks Protection Fund/Parks Pass Purchase	• 423	
Protect Our Coast and Oceans Fund	• 424	
Keep Arts in Schools Fund	• 425	
State Children's Trust Fund for the Prevention of Child Abuse	• 430	
Prevention of Animal Homelessness and Cruelty Fund	• 431	
Revive the Salton Sea Fund	• 432	
California Domestic Violence Victims Fund	• 433	
Special Olympics Fund	• 434	
Type 1 Diabetes Research Fund	• 435	
110 Add code 400 through code 435. This is your total contribution	• 110	

Your name [redacted] Your SSN or ITIN [redacted]

Amount You Owe

111 **AMOUNT YOU OWE.** If you do not have an amount on line 96, add line 93, line 97, and line 110. See instructions. **Do not send cash**

Mail to: FRANCHISE TAX BOARD
PO BOX 942867
SACRAMENTO CA 94267-0001 . . . . • 111 2,052.

Pay online – Go to ftb.ca.gov for more information.

Interest and Penalties

112 Interest, late return penalties, and late payment penalties 112

113 Underpayment of estimated tax. Check the box: • [X] FTB 5805 attached • [ ] FTB 5805F attached • 113 42.

114 Total amount due. See instructions. Enclose, but **do not** staple, any payment . . . . . 114 2,094.

Refund and Direct Deposit

115 **REFUND OR NO AMOUNT DUE.** Subtract the sum of line 110, line 112 and line 113 from line 96. See instructions.

Mail to: FRANCHISE TAX BOARD
PO BOX 942840
SACRAMENTO CA 94240-0001 . . . . • 115 0.

Fill in the information to authorize direct deposit of your refund into one or two accounts. **Do not attach a voided check or a deposit slip.** See instructions.

Have you verified the routing and account numbers? Use whole dollars only.

All or the following amount of my refund (line 115) is authorized for direct deposit into the account shown below:

• Routing number • Type: [ ] Checking [ ] Savings • Account number • 116 Direct deposit amount

The remaining amount of my refund (line 115) is authorized for direct deposit into the account shown below:

• Routing number • Type: [ ] Checking [ ] Savings • Account number • 117 Direct deposit amount

IMPORTANT: See the instructions to find out if you should attach a copy of your complete federal tax return.

To learn about your privacy rights, how we may use your information, and the consequences for not providing the requested information, go to ftb.ca.gov and search for privacy notice. To request this notice by mail, call 800.852.5711. Under penalties of perjury, I declare that I have examined this tax return, including accompanying schedules and statements, and to the best of my knowledge and belief, it is true, correct, and complete.

Your signature | Date | Spouse's/RDP's signature (if a joint tax return, both must sign)

Sign Here

It is unlawful to forge a spouse's/RDP's signature.

Joint tax return? (See instructions)

Your email address. Enter only one email address. | Preferred phone number: 650-515-1208

Paid preparer's signature (declaration of preparer is based on all information of which preparer has any knowledge)

Lucina V. delosReyes 9/1/17

Firm's name (or yours, if self-employed) | • PTIN
LUCINA V DE LOS REYES | P01204841

Firm's address | • FEIN
1529 HAMPTON COURT NAPERVILLE, IL 60565 | 27-2432384

Do you want to allow another person to discuss this tax return with us? See instructions . . . . . • [ ] Yes [X] No

Print Third Party Designee's Name | Telephone Number

031 3105164 Form 540 C1 2016 Side 5

TAXABLE YEAR **2016**

Underpayment of Estimated Tax by Individuals and Fiduciaries

CALIFORNIA FORM **5805**

Attach this form to Side 2 of your Form 540, Long Form 540NR, or Form 541. Also, check the box for underpayment of estimated tax located on Form 540, line 113; Long Form 540NR, line 123; or Form 541, line 44, whichever applies.

Name(s) as shown on return	SSN, ITIN, or FEIN
JOSE CAPISTRANO	318-94-4769

IMPORTANT: In most cases, the Franchise Tax Board (FTB) can figure the penalty for you and you do not have to complete this form. See General Information B.

If you meet any of the following conditions, you do not owe a penalty for underpayment of estimated tax. **Do not complete or file this form if:**

- The amount of your tax liability (not including tax on lump-sum distributions and accumulation distribution of trusts) less credits (including the withholding credit) but not including estimated tax payments for either 2015 or 2016 was less than $500 (or less than $250 if married/RDP filing a separate return).
- Your 2015 return was for a full 12 months (or would have been if you were required to file) and you did not have any tax liability on that return.
- The amount of your withholding plus your estimated tax payments, **if paid in the required installments**, is at least 90% of the tax shown on your 2016 return or 100% of the tax shown on your 2015 return (110% if California adjusted gross income (AGI) was more than $150,000 or $75,000 if married/RDP filing a separate return) and you are not using the annualized income installment method. Taxpayers with California AGI equal to or greater than $1,000,000 (or $500,000 if married/RDP filing a separate return), must use the tax shown on their 2016 tax return if they do not meet one of the two conditions above.

Part I **Questions.** All filers must complete this part. Estates and Trusts, see General Information E.

1 Are you requesting a waiver of the penalty? If "Yes," provide an explanation below and be sure to check the box on Form 540, line 113; Long Form 540NR, line 123; or Form 541, line 44. If you need additional space, attach a statement. See General Information C. . . . . . . 1 ☐ Yes ☒ No

2 Did you use the annualized income installment method? If "Yes," see instructions for Part III and be sure to check the box on Form 540, line 113; Long Form 540NR, line 123; or Form 541, line 44. . . . . . . 2 ☐ Yes ☒ No

3 Was your California withholding not withheld in equal installments and are you able to show the actual amounts withheld per period and the actual dates withheld? . . . . 3 ☐ Yes ☒ No ☐ N/A

If "Yes," enter the actual uneven amounts withheld on the spaces provided below. The total of the four amounts must equal the total withholding reported on Form 540, line 71 and line 73; Form 540NR, line 81 and line 83; or Form 541, line 29 and line 31.

4/15/16 $ ______ ; 6/15/16 $ ______ ; 9/15/16 $ ______ ; 1/15/17 $ ______

4 For estates and trusts: Was the date of death less than two years from the end of the taxable year? See General Information E. . . . 4 ☐ Yes ☐ No

For Privacy Notice, get FTB 1131 ENG/SP. 031 7671164 FTB 5805 2016 Side 1

rt II Required Annual Payment. All filers must complete this part.

1	Current year tax. Enter your 2016 tax after credits. See instructions		1	2,052.
2	Multiply line 1 by 90% (.90)	2	1,847.	
3	Withholding taxes. Do not include any estimated tax payments on this line. See instructions		3	
4	Subtract line 3 from line 1. If less than $500 (or less than $250 if married/RDP filing a separate return), stop here. You do not owe the penalty. Do not file form FTB 5805		4	2,052.
5	Enter the tax shown on your 2015 tax return. See instructions. (110% (1.10) of that amount if the adjusted gross income shown on that return is more than $150,000, or if married/RDP filing a separate return for 2016, more than $75,000)		5	2,241.
6	Required annual payment. Enter the smaller of line 2 or line 5. (If your California AGI is equal to or greater than $1,000,000/$500,000 for married/RDP filing a separate return, use line 2)		6	1,847.

ort Method

ution: See the instructions to find out if you can use the short method. If you answered "Yes" to Question 2 in Part I, skip this part and go to Part III. If you answered "No" to Question 2 in Part I and you cannot use the short method, go to Worksheet II in the instructions.

7	Enter the amount, if any, from Part II, line 3 above	7		
8	Enter the total amount, if any, of estimated tax payments you made	8		
9	Add line 7 and line 8		9	
10	Total underpayment for the year. Subtract line 9 from line 6. If zero or less, stop here. You do not owe the penalty. Do not file form FTB 5805		10	1,847.
11	Multiply line 10 by .02289425		11	42.
12	• If the amount on line 10 was paid on or after 4/15/17, enter -0-. • If the amount on line 10 was paid before 4/15/17, enter the result of the following computation: Amount on line 10 X Number of days paid before 4/15/17 X .00010		12	
13	PENALTY. Subtract line 12 from line 11. Enter the result here and on Form 540, line 113; Long Form 540NR, line 123; or Form 541, line 44. Also, check the box for "FTB 5805." ▶ ◉		13	42.

Form **1040** Department of the Treasury—Internal Revenue Service (99)
U.S. Individual Income Tax Return 2015

OMB No. 1545-0074 | IRS Use Only—Do not write or staple in this space. **FILE COPY**

For the year Jan. 1–Dec. 31, 2015, or other tax year beginning , ending | See separate instructions.

Your first name and initial	Last name	Your social security number
[redacted]	[redacted]	[redacted]
If a joint return, spouse's first name and initial	Last name	Spouse's social security number
Home address (number and street). If you have a P.O. box, see instructions. [redacted]	Apt. no. [redacted]	▲ Make sure the SSN(s) above and on line 6c are correct.
City, town or post office, state, and ZIP code. If you have a foreign address, also complete spaces below (see instructions). [redacted]		**Presidential Election Campaign** Check here if you, or your spouse if filing jointly, want $3 to go to this fund. Checking a box below will not change your tax or refund. ☐ You ☐ Spouse
Foreign country name	Foreign province/state/county	Foreign postal code

Filing Status

Check only one box.

1 ☒ Single
2 ☐ Married filing jointly (even if only one had income)
3 ☐ Married filing separately. Enter spouse's SSN above and full name here. ▶
4 ☐ Head of household (with qualifying person). (See instructions.) If the qualifying person is a child but not your dependent, enter this child's name here. ▶
5 ☐ Qualifying widow(er) with dependent child

Exemptions

6a ☒ **Yourself.** If someone can claim you as a dependent, **do not** check box 6a
b ☐ **Spouse**

Boxes checked on 6a and 6b: 1

c **Dependents:**

(1) First name Last name	(2) Dependent's social security number	(3) Dependent's relationship to you	(4) ✓ if child under age 17 qualifying for child tax credit (see instr.)
			☐
			☐
			☐
			☐

If more than four dependents, see instructions and check here ▶ ☐

No. of children on 6c who:
• lived with you: 0
• did not live with you due to divorce or separation (see instructions): 0
Dependents on 6c not entered above: 0

d Total number of exemptions claimed — Add numbers on lines above ▶ 1

Income

Attach Form(s) W-2 here. Also attach Forms W-2G and 1099-R if tax was withheld.

If you did not get a W-2, see instructions.

7	Wages, salaries, tips, etc. Attach Form(s) W-2	7	17,485.
8a	**Taxable** interest. Attach Schedule B if required	8a	
b	**Tax-exempt** interest. **Do not** include on line 8a — 8b		
9a	Ordinary dividends. Attach Schedule B if required	9a	
b	Qualified dividends — 9b		
10	Taxable refunds, credits, or offsets of state and local income taxes	10	
11	Alimony received	11	
12	Business income or (loss). Attach Schedule C or C-EZ	12	51,000.
13	Capital gain or (loss). Attach Schedule D if required. If not required, check here ▶ ☐	13	
14	Other gains or (losses). Attach Form 4797	14	
15a	IRA distributions — 15a — b Taxable amount	15b	
16a	Pensions and annuities — 16a — b Taxable amount	16b	
17	Rental real estate, royalties, partnerships, S corporations, trusts, etc. Attach Schedule E	17	
18	Farm income or (loss). Attach Schedule F	18	
19	Unemployment compensation	19	
20a	Social security benefits — 20a — b Taxable amount	20b	
21	Other income. List type and amount	21	
22	Combine the amounts in the far right column for lines 7 through 21. This is your **total income** ▶	22	68,485.

Adjusted Gross Income

23	Educator expenses	23			
24	Certain business expenses of reservists, performing artists, and fee-basis government officials. Attach Form 2106 or 2106-EZ	24			
25	Health savings account deduction. Attach Form 8889	25			
26	Moving expenses. Attach Form 3903	26			
27	Deductible part of self-employment tax. Attach Schedule SE	27	3,603.		
28	Self-employed SEP, SIMPLE, and qualified plans	28			
29	Self-employed health insurance deduction	29	8,400.		
30	Penalty on early withdrawal of savings	30			
31a	Alimony paid b Recipient's SSN ▶	31a			
32	IRA deduction	32			
33	Student loan interest deduction	33			
34	Tuition and fees. Attach Form 8917	34			
35	Domestic production activities deduction. Attach Form 8903	35			
36	Add lines 23 through 35			36	12,003.
37	Subtract line 36 from line 22. This is your **adjusted gross income** ▶			37	56,482.

For Disclosure, Privacy Act, and Paperwork Reduction Act Notice, see separate instructions.

JWA Form **1040** (2015)

Tax and Credits	38	Amount from line 37 (adjusted gross income)	38	56,482.
	39a	Check if: [ ] You were born before January 2, 1951, [ ] Blind. [ ] Spouse was born before January 2, 1951, [ ] Blind. Total boxes checked ▶ 39a 0		
	b	If your spouse itemizes on a separate return or you were a dual-status alien, check here ▶ 39b [ ]		
	40	Itemized deductions (from Schedule A) or your standard deduction (see left margin)	40	6,300.
	41	Subtract line 40 from line 38	41	50,182.
	42	Exemptions. If line 38 is $154,950 or less, multiply $4,000 by the number on line 6d. Otherwise, see instructions	42	4,000.
	43	Taxable income. Subtract line 42 from line 41. If line 42 is more than line 41, enter -0-	43	46,182.
	44	Tax (see instructions). Check if any from: a [ ] Form(s) 8814 b [ ] Form 4972 c [ ]	44	7,338.
	45	Alternative minimum tax (see instructions). Attach Form 6251	45	
	46	Excess advance premium tax credit repayment. Attach Form 8962	46	
	47	Add lines 44, 45, and 46 ▶	47	7,338.
	48	Foreign tax credit. Attach Form 1116 if required	48	
	49	Credit for child and dependent care expenses. Attach Form 2441	49	
	50	Education credits from Form 8863, line 19	50	
	51	Retirement savings contributions credit. Attach Form 8880	51	
	52	Child tax credit. Attach Schedule 8812, if required	52	
	53	Residential energy credits. Attach Form 5695	53	
	54	Other credits from Form: a [ ] 3800 b [ ] 8801 c [ ]	54	
	55	Add lines 48 through 54. These are your total credits	55	0.
	56	Subtract line 55 from line 47. If line 55 is more than line 47, enter -0- ▶	56	7,338.
Other Taxes	57	Self-employment tax. Attach Schedule SE	57	7,206.
	58	Unreported social security and Medicare tax from Form: a [ ] 4137 b [ ] 8919	58	
	59	Additional tax on IRAs, other qualified retirement plans, etc. Attach Form 5329 if required	59	
	60a	Household employment taxes from Schedule H	60a	
	b	First-time homebuyer credit repayment. Attach Form 5405 if required	60b	
	61	Health care: individual responsibility (see instructions) Full-year coverage [X]	61	
	62	Taxes from: a [ ] Form 8959 b [ ] Form 8960 c [ ] Instructions; enter code(s)	62	
	63	Add lines 56 through 62. This is your total tax ▶	63	14,544.
Payments	64	Federal income tax withheld from Forms W-2 and 1099	64	3,188.
	65	2015 estimated tax payments and amount applied from 2014 return	65	
	66a	Earned income credit (EIC) NO	66a	
	b	Nontaxable combat pay election 66b		
	67	Additional child tax credit. Attach Schedule 8812	67	
	68	American opportunity credit from Form 8863, line 8	68	
	69	Net premium tax credit. Attach Form 8962	69	
	70	Amount paid with request for extension to file	70	
	71	Excess social security and tier 1 RRTA tax withheld	71	
	72	Credit for federal tax on fuels. Attach Form 4136	72	
	73	Credits from Form: a [ ] 2439 b Reserved c [ ] 8885 d [ ]	73	
	74	Add lines 64, 65, 66a, and 67 through 73. These are your total payments ▶	74	3,188.
Refund	75	If line 74 is more than line 63, subtract line 63 from line 74. This is the amount you overpaid	75	0.
	76a	Amount of line 75 you want refunded to you. If Form 8888 is attached, check here ▶ [ ]	76a	0.
	▶ b	Routing number ▶ c Type: [ ] Checking [ ] Savings		
	▶ d	Account number		
	77	Amount of line 75 you want applied to your 2016 estimated tax ▶ 77		
Amount You Owe	78	Amount you owe. Subtract line 74 from line 63. For details on how to pay, see instructions ▶	78	11,554.
	79	Estimated tax penalty (see instructions) 79 198.		

Standard Deduction for— • People who check any box on line 39a or 39b or who can be claimed as a dependent, see instructions. • All others: Single or Married filing separately, $6,300; Married filing jointly or Qualifying widow(er), $12,600; Head of household, $9,250

If you have a qualifying child, attach Schedule EIC.

Direct deposit? See instructions.

Third Party Designee Do you want to allow another person to discuss this return with the IRS (see instructions)? [ ] Yes. Complete below. [X] No
Designee's name ▶ Phone no. ▶ Personal identification number (PIN) ▶

Sign Here Under penalties of perjury, I declare that I have examined this return and accompanying schedules and statements, and to the best of my knowledge and belief, they are true, correct, and complete. Declaration of preparer (other than taxpayer) is based on all information of which preparer has any knowledge.

Joint return? See instr. Keep a copy for your records.

Your signature	Date	Your occupation	Daytime phone number
		Travel Phy. Therap.	
Spouse's signature. If a joint return, both must sign.	Date	Spouse's occupation	If the IRS sent you an Identity Protection PIN, enter it here (see inst.)

Paid Preparer Use Only

Print/Type preparer's name	Preparer's signature	Date	Check [X] if self-employed	PTIN
Lucina V de los Reyes	Lucina V. delos Reyes	4/10/16		P01204841

Firm's name ▶ Lucina V de los Reyes — Firm's EIN ▶ 27-2432384
Firm's address ▶ 1529 Hampton Court, Naperville, IL 60565 — Phone no. (630)983-6227

SCHEDULE C (Form 1040) Department of the Treasury Internal Revenue Service (99)	**Profit or Loss From Business** (Sole Proprietorship) ▶ Information about Schedule C and its separate instructions is at www.irs.gov/schedulec. ▶ Attach to Form 1040, 1040NR, or 1041; partnerships generally must file Form 1065.	OMB No. 1545-0074 **2015** Attachment Sequence No. 09

Name of proprietor [redacted] — Social security number (SSN) [redacted]

A Principal business or profession, including product or service (see instructions): Travelling Physical Therapist — B Enter code from instructions ▶ [redacted]

C Business name. If no separate business name, leave blank. — D Employer ID number (EIN), (see instr.)

E Business address (including suite or room no.) ▶

City, town or post office, state, and ZIP code

F Accounting method: (1) [X] Cash (2) [ ] Accrual (3) [ ] Other (specify) ▶

G Did you "materially participate" in the operation of this business during 2015? If "No," see instructions for limit on losses . . . . . [X] Yes [ ] No

H If you started or acquired this business during 2015, check here . . . . . ▶ [ ]

I Did you make any payments in 2015 that would require you to file Form(s) 1099? (see instructions) . . . . . [ ] Yes [ ] No

J If "Yes," did you or will you file required Forms 1099? . . . . . [ ] Yes [ ] No

Part I Income

1	Gross receipts or sales. See instructions for line 1 and check the box if this income was reported to you on Form W-2 and the "Statutory employee" box on that form was checked . . . ▶ [ ]	1	137,690.
2	Returns and allowances	2	
3	Subtract line 2 from line 1	3	137,690.
4	Cost of goods sold (from line 42)	4	
5	**Gross profit.** Subtract line 4 from line 3	5	137,690.
6	Other income, including federal and state gasoline or fuel tax credit or refund (see instructions)	6	
7	**Gross income.** Add lines 5 and 6 ▶	7	137,690.

Part II Expenses. Enter expenses for business use of your home only on line 30.

		Line	Amount			Line	Amount
8	Advertising	8		18	Office expense (see instructions)	18	
9	Car and truck expenses (see instructions)	9	34,500.	19	Pension and profit-sharing plans	19	
10	Commissions and fees	10		20	Rent or lease (see instructions):		
11	Contract labor (see instructions)	11		a	Vehicles, machinery, and equipment	20a	
12	Depletion	12		b	Other business property	20b	
13	Depreciation and section 179 expense deduction (not included in Part III) (see instructions)	13		21	Repairs and maintenance	21	1,040.
14	Employee benefit programs (other than on line 19)	14		22	Supplies (not included in Part III)	22	2,500.
15	Insurance (other than health)	15	2,400.	23	Taxes and licenses	23	
16	Interest:			24	Travel, meals, and entertainment:		
a	Mortgage (paid to banks, etc.)	16a		a	Travel	24a	20,000.
b	Other	16b		b	Deductible meals and entertainment (see instructions)	24b	
17	Legal and professional services	17	17,200.	25	Utilities	25	
				26	Wages (less employment credits)	26	
				27a	Other expenses (from line 48)	27a	9,050.
				b	Reserved for future use	27b	

28	**Total expenses** before expenses for business use of home. Add lines 8 through 27a ▶	28	86,690.
29	Tentative profit or (loss). Subtract line 28 from line 7	29	51,000.
30	Expenses for business use of your home. Do not report these expenses elsewhere. Attach Form 8829 unless using the simplified method (see instructions). **Simplified method filers only:** enter the total square footage of: (a) your home: ____ and (b) the part of your home used for business: ____. Use the Simplified Method Worksheet in the instructions to figure the amount to enter on line 30	30	
31	**Net profit or (loss).** Subtract line 30 from line 29. • If a profit, enter on both **Form 1040, line 12** (or **Form 1040NR, line 13**) and on **Schedule SE, line 2.** (If you checked the box on line 1, see instructions). Estates and trusts, enter on **Form 1041, line 3.** • If a loss, you **must** go to line 32.	31	51,000.
32	If you have a loss, check the box that describes your investment in this activity (see instructions). • If you checked 32a, enter the loss on both **Form 1040, line 12,** (or **Form 1040NR, line 13**) and on **Schedule SE, line 2.** (If you checked the box on line 1, see the line 31 instructions). Estates and trusts, enter on **Form 1041, line 3.** • If you checked 32b, you **must** attach **Form 6198.** Your loss may be limited.	32a [ ] All investment is at risk. 32b [ ] Some investment is not at risk.	

For Paperwork Reduction Act Notice, see the separate instructions. — Schedule C (Form 1040) 2015

DYA

06/06/2016 08:08:56PM

Part III Cost of Goods Sold (see instructions)

33 Method(s) used to value closing inventory: a ☐ Cost b ☐ Lower of cost or market c ☐ Other (attach explanation)

34 Was there any change in determining quantities, costs, or valuations between opening and closing inventory? If "Yes," attach explanation ☐ Yes ☐ No

35	Inventory at beginning of year. If different from last year's closing inventory, attach explanation	35	
36	Purchases less cost of items withdrawn for personal use	36	
37	Cost of labor. Do not include any amounts paid to yourself	37	
38	Materials and supplies	38	
39	Other costs	39	
40	Add lines 35 through 39	40	
41	Inventory at end of year	41	
42	**Cost of goods sold.** Subtract line 41 from line 40. Enter the result here and on line 4	42	0.

Part IV Information on Your Vehicle. Complete this part **only** if you are claiming car or truck expenses on line 9 and are not required to file Form 4562 for this business. See the instructions for line 13 to find out if you must file Form 4562.

43 When did you place your vehicle in service for business purposes? (month, day, year) ▶ 02/25/2002

44 Of the total number of miles you drove your vehicle during 2015, enter the number of miles you used your vehicle for:

a Business 60000 b Commuting (see instructions) 0 c Other 0

45 Was your vehicle available for personal use during off-duty hours? ☒ Yes ☐ No

46 Do you (or your spouse) have another vehicle available for personal use? ☒ Yes ☐ No

47a Do you have evidence to support your deduction? ☐ Yes ☐ No

b If "Yes," is the evidence written? ☐ Yes ☐ No

Part V Other Expenses. List below business expenses not included on lines 8-26 or line 30.

Uniform/upkeep	1,500.
Cellphone, Phone bills	2,400.
Internet	1,500.
PT tools	2,450.
Car registration	700.
Parking fees/tolls	500.
48 **Total other expenses.** Enter here and on line 27a — 48	9,050.

SCHEDULE SE (Form 1040) Department of the Treasury Internal Revenue Service (99)	**Self-Employment Tax** ▶ Information about Schedule SE and its separate instructions is at *www.irs.gov/schedulese.* ▶ Attach to Form 1040 or Form 1040NR.	OMB No. 1545-0074 **2015** Attachment Sequence No. 17

Name of person with self-employment income (as shown on Form 1040 or Form 1040NR)	Social security number of person with self-employment income ▶
[redacted]	[redacted]

Before you begin: To determine if you must file Schedule SE, see the instructions.

May I Use Short Schedule SE or Must I Use Long Schedule SE?

Note. Use this flowchart **only if** you must file Schedule SE. If unsure, see *Who Must File Schedule SE* in the instructions.

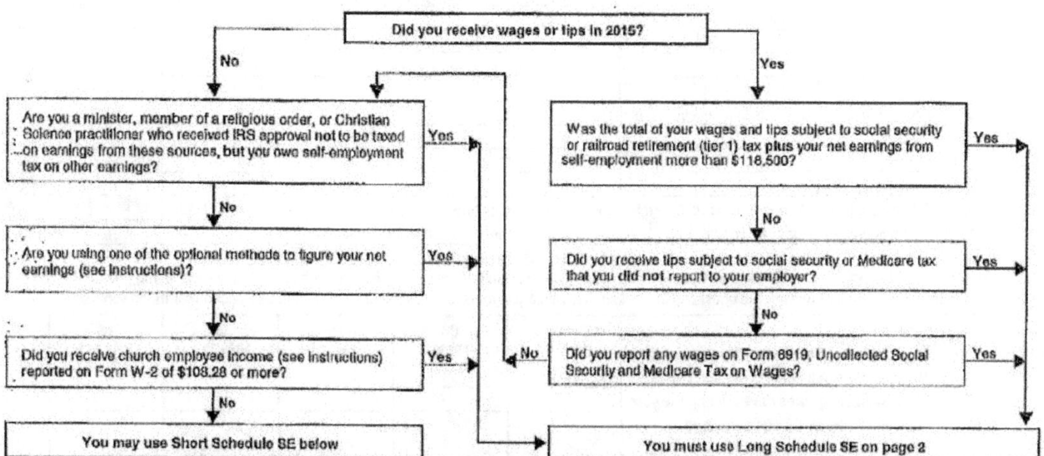

Section A - Short Schedule SE. Caution. Read above to see if you can use Short Schedule SE.

1a	Net farm profit or (loss) from Schedule F, line 34, and farm partnerships, Schedule K-1 (Form 1065), box 14, code A	1a	
b	If you received social security retirement or disability benefits, enter the amount of Conservation Reserve Program payments included on Schedule F, line 4b, or listed on Schedule K-1 (Form 1065), box 20, code Z	1b	( )
2	Net profit or (loss) from Schedule C, line 31; Schedule C-EZ, line 3; Schedule K-1 (Form 1065), box 14, code A (other than farming); and Schedule K-1 (Form 1065-B), box 9, code J1. Ministers and members of religious orders, see instructions for types of income to report on this line. See instructions for other income to report	2	51,000.
3	Combine lines 1a, 1b, and 2	3	51,000.
4	Multiply line 3 by 92.35% (.9235). If less than $400, you do not owe self-employment tax; **do not** file this schedule unless you have an amount on line 1b . . . . . ▶ **Note.** If line 4 is less than $400 due to Conservation Reserve Program payments on line 1b, see instructions.	4	47,099.
5	**Self-employment tax.** If the amount on line 4 is: • $118,500 or less, multiply line 4 by 15.3% (.153). Enter the result here and on **Form 1040, line 57,** or **Form 1040NR, line 55** • More than $118,500, multiply line 4 by 2.9% (.029). Then, add $14,694 to the result. Enter the total here and on **Form 1040, line 57,** or **Form 1040NR, line 55**	5	7,206.
6	**Deduction for one-half of self-employment tax.** Multiply line 5 by 50% (.50). Enter the result here and on **Form 1040, line 27,** or **Form 1040NR, line 27** . . . . . 6 | 3,603.		

For Paperwork Reduction Act Notice, see your tax return instructions. UYA **Schedule SE (Form 1040) 2015**

Part V **Listed Property** (Include automobiles, certain other vehicles, certain aircraft, certain computers, and property used for entertainment, recreation, or amusement.)

Note: *For any vehicle for which you are using the standard mileage rate or deducting lease expense, complete* ***only*** *24a, 24b, columns (a) through (c) of Section A, all of Section B, and Section C if applicable.*

Section A—Depreciation and Other Information (Caution: See the instructions for limits for passenger automobiles)

24a Do you have evidence to support the business/investment use claimed? ☐ Yes ☐ No **24b** If "Yes," is the evidence written? ☐ Yes ☐ No

(a) Type of property (list vehicles first)	(b) Date placed in service	(c) Business/ investment use percentage	(d) Cost or other basis	(e) Basis for depreciation (business/investment use only)	(f) Recovery period	(g) Method/ Convention	(h) Depreciation deduction	(i) Elected section 179 cost
25 Special depreciation allowance for qualified listed property placed in service during the tax year and used more than 50% in a qualified business use (see instructions) 25								
26 Property used more than 50% in a qualified business use:								
Car	02/25/02	100.0%						
		%						
		%						
27 Property used 50% or less in a qualified business use:								
		%				S/L -		
		%				S/L -		
		%				S/L -		
28 Add amounts in column (h), lines 25 through 27. Enter here and on line 21, page 1 28								
29 Add amounts in column (i), line 26. Enter here and on line 7, page 1 29								

Section B—Information on Use of Vehicles

Complete this section for vehicles used by a sole proprietor, partner, or other "more than 5% owner," or related person. If you provided vehicles to your employees, first answer the questions in Section C to see if you meet an exception to completing this section for those vehicles.

	(a) Vehicle 1 (Car)		(b) Vehicle 2		(c) Vehicle 3		(d) Vehicle 4		(e) Vehicle 5		(f) Vehicle 6	
30 Total business/investment miles driven during the year (do not include commuting miles) .	60000											
31 Total commuting miles driven during the year												
32 Total other personal (noncommuting) miles driven												
33 Total miles driven during the year. Add lines 30 through 32	60000											
	Yes	No	Yes	No	Yes	No	Yes	No	Yes	No	Yes	No
34 Was the vehicle available for personal use during off-duty hours?	X											
35 Was the vehicle used primarily by a more than 5% owner or related person? . . .	X											
36 Is another vehicle available for personal use?	X											

Section C—Questions for Employers Who Provide Vehicles for Use by Their Employees

Answer these questions to determine if you meet an exception to completing Section B for vehicles used by employees who **are not** more than 5% owners or related persons (see instructions).

	Yes	No
37 Do you maintain a written policy statement that prohibits all personal use of vehicles, including commuting, by your employees?		
38 Do you maintain a written policy statement that prohibits personal use of vehicles, except commuting, by your employees? See the instructions for vehicles used by corporate officers, directors, or 1% or more owners		
39 Do you treat all use of vehicles by employees as personal use?		
40 Do you provide more than five vehicles to your employees, obtain information from your employees about the use of the vehicles, and retain the information received?		
41 Do you meet the requirements concerning qualified automobile demonstration use? (See instructions.)		

Note: *If your answer to 37, 38, 39, 40, or 41 is "Yes," do not complete Section B for the covered vehicles.*

Part VI **Amortization**

(a) Description of costs	(b) Date amortization begins	(c) Amortizable amount	(d) Code section	(e) Amortization period or percentage	(f) Amortization for this year
42 Amortization of costs that begins during your 2015 tax year (see instructions):					
43 Amortization of costs that began before your 2015 tax year 43					
44 **Total.** Add amounts in column (f). See the instructions for where to report 44					

FORM

2015 California Resident Income Tax Return **540**

APE

ATTACH FEDERAL RETURN

A

15 PBA 621610

R

RP

FILE COPY

08-06-1971

Filing Status

1 [X] Single
2 [ ] Married/RDP filing jointly. See inst.
3 [ ] Married/RDP filing separately. Enter spouse's/RDP's SSN or ITIN above and full name here
4 [ ] Head of household (with qualifying person). See instructions.
5 [ ] Qualifying widow(er) with dependent child. Enter year spouse/RDP died.

If your California filing status is different from your federal filing status, check the box here . . . . [ ]

6 If someone can claim you (or your spouse/RDP) as a dependent, check the box here. See instructions . . . . ● 6 [ ]

Exemptions

For line 7, line 8, line 9, and line 10: Multiply the amount you enter in the box by the pre-printed dollar amount for that line. **Whole dollars only**

7 **Personal:** If you checked box 1, 3, or 4 above, enter 1 in the box. If you checked box 2 or 5, enter 2 in the box. If you checked the box on line 6, see instructions ● 7 [1] X $109 = ● $ 109.

8 **Blind:** If you (or your spouse/RDP) are visually impaired, enter 1; if both are visually impaired, enter 2 . . . . ● 8 [ ] X $109 = ● $

9 **Senior:** If you (or your spouse/RDP) are 65 or older, enter 1; if both are 65 or older, enter 2 . . . . ● 9 [ ] X $109 = ● $

10 **Dependents: Do not include yourself or your spouse/RDP.**

	Dependent 1	Dependent 2	Dependent 3
First name			
Last name			
SSN			
Dependent's relationship to you			

Total dependent exemptions . . . . ● 10 [ ] X $337 = ● $

11 **Exemption amount:** Add line 7 through line 10. Transfer this amount to line 32. . . . . ● 11 $ 109.

Your name: [redacted] Your SSN or ITIN: [redacted]

Taxable Income

12	State wages from your Form(s) W-2, box 16	12	17,485.
13	Enter federal adjusted gross income from Form 1040, line 37; 1040A, line 21; or 1040EZ, line 4	13	56,482.
14	California adjustments - subtractions. Enter the amount from Schedule CA (540), line 37, column B	14	
15	Subtract line 14 from line 13. If less than zero, enter the result in parentheses. See instructions	15	56,482.
16	California adjustments - additions. Enter the amount from Schedule CA (540), line 37, column C	16	
17	California adjusted gross income. Combine line 15 and line 16	17	56,482.
18	Enter the larger of: Your California **itemized deductions** from Schedule CA (540), line 44; OR Your California **standard deduction** shown below for your filing status: • Single or Married/RDP filing separately . . . $4,044 • Married/RDP filing jointly, Head of household, or Qualifying widow(er) . . $8,088 If the box on line 6 is checked, STOP. See instructions	18	4,044.
19	Subtract line 18 from line 17. This is your **taxable income**. If less than zero, enter -0-	19	52,438.

Tax

31	Tax. Check box if from: [X] Tax Table [ ] Tax Rate Schedule [ ] FTB 3800 [ ] FTB 3803	31	2,350.
32	Exemption credits. Enter the amount from line 11. If your federal AGI is more than $178,706, see instr.	32	109.
33	Subtract line 32 from line 31. If less than zero, enter -0-	33	2,241.
34	Tax. See instructions. Check box if from: [ ] Schedule G-1 [ ] Form FTB 5870A	34	
35	Add line 33 and line 34	35	2,241.

Special Credits

40	Nonrefundable Child and Dependent Care Expenses Credit. See instructions	40	
43	Enter credit name ______ code ______ and amount	43	
44	Enter credit name ______ code ______ and amount	44	
45	To claim more than two credits, see instructions. Attach Schedule P (540)	45	
46	Nonrefundable renter's credit. See instructions	46	
47	Add line 40 through line 46. These are your total credits	47	0.
48	Subtract line 47 from line 35. If less than zero, enter -0-	48	2,241.

Other Taxes

61	Alternative minimum tax. Attach Schedule P (540)	61	
62	Mental Health Services Tax. See instructions	62	
63	Other taxes and credit recapture. See instructions	63	
64	Add line 48, line 61, line 62, and line 63. This is your total tax	64	2,241.

Your name: [redacted] Your SSN or ITIN: [redacted]

Section	Line	Description		Amount
Payments	71	California income tax withheld. See instructions	71	981.
	72	2015 CA estimated tax and other payments. See instructions	72	
	73	Withholding (Form 592-B and/or 593). See instructions	73	
	74	Excess SDI (or VPDI) withheld. See instructions	74	
	75	Earned Income Tax Credit (EITC)	75	
	76	Add lines 71 through 75. These are your total payments. See instructions	76	981.
Use Tax	91	Use Tax. **This is not a total line. See instructions.**	91	
Overpaid Tax/ Tax Due	92	Payments balance. If line 76 is more than line 91, subtract line 91 from line 76	92	981.
	93	**Use Tax balance.** If line 91 is more than line 76, subtract line 76 from line 91	93	
	94	Overpaid tax. If line 92 is more than line 64, subtract line 64 from line 92	94	
	95	Amount of line 94 you want applied to your 2016 estimated tax	95	
	96	Overpaid tax avaible this year. Subtract line 95 from 94	96	
	97	Tax due. If line 92 is less than line 64, subtract line 92 from line 64	97	1,260.

Your name: [redacted] Your SSN or ITIN: [redacted]

Contributions

	Code	Amount
California Seniors Special Fund. See instructions	• 400	
Alzheimer's Disease/Related Disorders Fund	• 401	
Rare and Endangered Species Preservation Program	• 403	
California Breast Cancer Research Fund	• 405	
California Firefighters' Memorial Fund	• 406	
Emergency Food for Families Fund	• 407	
California Peace Officer Memorial Foundation Fund	• 408	
California Sea Otter Fund	• 410	
California Cancer Research Fund	• 413	
Child Victims of Human Trafficking Fund	• 419	
School Supplies for Homeless Children Fund	• 422	
State Parks Protection Fund/Parks Pass Purchase	• 423	
Protect Our Coast and Oceans Fund	• 424	
Keep Arts in Schools Fund	• 425	
California Senior Legislature Fund	• 427	
Habitat for Humanity Fund	• 428	
California Sexual Violence Victim Services Fund	• 429	
State Children's Trust Fund for the Prevention of Child Abuse	• 430	
Prevention of Animal Homelessness & Cruelty Fund	• 431	
110 Add code 400 through code 431. This is your total contribution	• 110	

Your name: [redacted] Your SSN or ITIN: [redacted]

Amount You Owe

111 **AMOUNT YOU OWE.** If you do not have an amount on line 96, add line 93, line 97, and line 110. See instructions. **Do not send cash.**
Mail to: **FRANCHISE TAX BOARD**
PO BOX 942867
SACRAMENTO CA 94267-0001 . . . . ● 111 | 1,260.
Pay online – Go to **ftb.ca.gov** for more information.

Interest and Penalties

112 Interest, late return penalties, and late payment penalties 112

113 Underpayment of estimated tax. Check the box: ● [X] FTB 5805 attached ● [ ] FTB 5805F attached ● 113

114 Total amount due. See instructions. Enclose, but do not staple, any payment. . . . . 114 | 1,260.

Refund and Direct Deposit

115 **REFUND OR NO AMOUNT DUE.** Subtract the sum of line 110, and line 112 from line 113 from line 96. See instructions
Mail to: **FRANCHISE TAX BOARD**
PO BOX 942840
SACRAMENTO CA 94240-0001 . . . . ● 115 | 0.

Fill in the information to authorize direct deposit of your refund into one or two accounts. **Do not attach a voided check or a deposit slip.** See instructions
Have you verified the routing and account numbers? Use whole dollars only.
All or the following amount of my refund (line 115) is authorized for direct deposit into the account shown below:

● Routing number | ● Type [ ] Checking [ ] Savings | ● Account number | ● 116 Direct deposit amount

The remaining amount of my refund (line 115) is authorized for direct deposit into the account shown below:

● Routing number | ● Type [ ] Checking [ ] Savings | ● Account number | ● 117 Direct deposit amount

IMPORTANT: See the instructions to find out if you should attach a copy of your complete federal tax return.

To learn about your privacy rights, how we may use your information, and the consequences for not providing the requested information, got to **ftb.ca.gov** and search for **privacy notice.** To request this notice by mail, call 800.852.5711. Under penalties of perjury, I declare that I have examined this tax return, including accompanying schedules and statements, and to the best of my knowledge and belief, it is true, correct, and complete.

Sign Here

It is unlawful to forge a spouse's/RDP's signature.

Joint tax return? (See instructions.)

Your signature | Date | Spouse's/RDP's signature (if a joint tax return, both must sign)

Your email address (optional). Enter only one email address. | Daytime phone number (optional) [redacted]

Paid preparer's signature (declaration of preparer is based on all information of which preparer has any knowledge)

Lucina V. de los Reyes

Firm's name (or yours, if self-employed) [redacted] | ● PTIN [redacted]

Firm's address [redacted] | ● FEIN [redacted]

Do you want to allow another person to discuss this tax return with us? See instructions . . . . ● [ ] Yes [X] No

Print Third Party Designee's Name | Telephone Number

TAXABLE YEAR

2015

Wage and Tax Statement

CALIFORNIA SCHEDULE

W-2

Important: Attach this form to the back of your Form 540, 540 2EZ, or Form 540NR (Long or Short).

Name(s) as shown on tax return

SSN or ITIN

Caution: If this form is filled out, **do not** send your Form(s) W-2 to the Franchise Tax Board. If your Form(s) W-2 are from multiple states, **attach** copies showing California tax withheld to this schedule. If this schedule is blank, attach your Form(s) W-2 to the lower front of your tax return.

All fields must be completed. DO NOT ATTACH PAYMENT TO THIS SCHEDULE.

* Employee's social security number, name, and address must be the same as the information on the Form(s) W-2.

W-2 Information	1st W-2	2nd W-2
a. Employee's social security number *		
b. Employer identification number (EIN)		
c. Employer's name	HARDEN HOME HEALTH	CALCARE HOME HEALTH CARE
Address	12900 FOSTER	455 HICKEY BLVD
City	OVERLAND PARK	DALY CITY
State	KS	CA
Zip code	66213	94015
e. Employee's first name*		JOSE
Middle initial*		
Last name*		
Suffix*		
f. Employee address*		
City*	SAN MATEO	
State*	CA	
Zip code*	94401	
1. Wages, tips, other compensation	16,285.	1,200.
2. Federal income tax withheld	3,042.	146.
3. Social security wages	16,285.	1,200.
4. Social security tax withheld	1,010.	74.
6. Medicare tax withheld	236.	17.

W-2 Information	1st W-2		2nd W-2	
7. Social security tips				
8. Allocated tips (not included in box 1)				
10. Dependent care benefits				
11. Nonqualified plans				
12. Codes and amounts	Codes	Amounts	Codes	Amounts
12a.				
12b.				
12c.				
12d.				
13. Check the appropriate box for: Statutory employee, Retirement plan, or Third-party sick pay	☐ Statutory employee ☐ Retirement plan ☐ Third-party sick pay		☐ Statutory employee ☐ Retirement plan ☐ Third-party sick pay	
14. SDI, VPDI, or CA SDI (from box 14 or 19)	Type: CA SDI	Amount: 147.	Type: CA SDI	Amount: 11.
15. State and employer's State ID number	State: CA	Employer's state ID number: 010-6263-7	State: CA	Employer's state ID number: 004-6412-3
16. State wages, tips, etc.	16,285.		1,200.	
17. State income tax	956.		25.	

TAXABLE YEAR **2015**

Underpayment of Estimated Tax by Individuals and Fiduciaries

CALIFORNIA FORM **5805**

Attach this form to **Side 2** of your Form 540, Long Form 540NR, or Form 541. Also, check the box for underpayment of estimated tax located on Form 540, line 113; Long Form 540NR, line 123; or Form 541, line 44, whichever applies.

Name(s) as shown on return

SSN, ITIN, or FEIN

IMPORTANT: In most cases, the Franchise Tax Board (FTB) can figure the penalty for you and you do not have to complete this form. See General Information B.

If you meet any of the following conditions, you do not owe a penalty for underpayment of estimated tax. **Do not complete or file this form if:**

- The amount of your tax liability (not including tax on lump-sum distributions and accumulation distribution of trusts) less credits (including the withholding credit) but not including estimated tax payments for either 2014 or 2015 was less than $500 (or less than $250 if married/RDP filing a separate return).
- Your 2014 return was for a full 12 months (or would have been if you were required to file) and you did not have any tax liability on that return.
- The amount of your withholding plus your estimated tax payments, **if paid in the required installments,** is at least 90% of the tax shown on your 2015 return or 100% of the tax shown on your 2014 return (110% if California adjusted gross income (AGI) was more than $150,000 or $75,000 if married/RDP filing a separate return) and you are not using the annualized income installment method. Taxpayers with California AGI equal to or greater than $1,000,000 (or $500,000 if married/RDP filing a separate return), must use the tax shown on their 2015 tax return if they do not meet one of the two conditions above.

Part I Questions. All filers must complete this part. Estates and Trusts, see General information E.

1 Are you requesting a waiver of the penalty? If "Yes," provide an explanation below and be sure to check the box on Form 540, line 113; Long Form 540NR, line 123; or Form 541, line 44. If you need additional space, attach a statement. See General Information C . . . . 1 ☒ Yes ☐ No

2 Did you use the annualized income installment method? If "Yes," see instructions for Part III and be sure to check the box on Form 540, line 113; Long Form 540NR, line 123; or Form 541, line 44. . . . . 2 ☐ Yes ☒ No

3 Was your California withholding not withheld in equal installments and are you able to show the actual amounts withheld per period and the actual dates withheld? . . . . 3 ☐ Yes ☒ No ☐ N/A

If "Yes," enter the **actual uneven amounts withheld** on the spaces provided below. The total of the four amounts must equal the total withholding reported on Form 540, line 71 and line 73; Form 540NR, line 81 and line 83; or Form 541, line 29 and line 31.

4/15/15 $______; 6/15/15 $______; 9/15/15 $______; 1/15/16 $______.

4 For estates and trusts: Was the date of death less than two years from the end of the taxable year? See General Information E . . . 4 ☐ Yes ☐ No

Part II Required Annual Payment. All filers must complete this part.

Line	Description	Amount
1	Current year tax. Enter your 2015 tax after credits. See instructions . . . 1	2,241.
2	Multiply line 1 by 90% (.90) . . . 2	2,017.
3	Withholding taxes. **Do not** include any estimated tax payments on this line. See instructions . . . 3	981.
4	Subtract line 3 from line 1. If less than $500 (or less than $250 if married/RDP filing a separate return), stop here. You do not owe the penalty. **Do not** file form FTB 5805 . . . 4	1,260.
5	Enter the tax shown on your 2014 tax return. **See instructions.** (110% (1.10) of that amount if the adjusted gross income shown on that return is more than $150,000, or if married/RDP filing a separate return for 2015, more than $75,000). 5	7,260.
6	Required annual payment. Enter the **smaller** of line 2 or line 5. (If your California AGI is equal to or greater than $1,000,000/$500,000 for married/RDP filing a separate return, use line 2) . . . 6	2,017.

Short Method

Caution: See the instructions to find out if you can use the short method. If you answered "Yes" to Question 2 in Part I, skip this part and go to Part III. If you answered "No" to Question 2 in Part I **and** you cannot use the short method, go to Worksheet II in the instructions.

Line	Description	Amount
7	Enter the amount, if any, from Part II, line 3 above . . . 7	981.
8	Enter the total amount, if any, of estimated tax payments you made . . . 8	
9	Add line 7 and line 8 . . . 9	981.
10	**Total underpayment for the year.** Subtract line 9 from line 6. If zero or less, stop here. You do not owe the penalty. **Do not file** form FTB 5805 . . . 10	1,036.
11	Multiply line 10 by .02126976 . . . 11	22.
12	• If the amount on line 10 was paid **on or after** 4/15/16, enter -0-. • If the amount on line 10 was paid **before** 4/15/16, enter the result of the following computation: Amount on line 10 X Number of days paid before 4/15/16 X .00008 . . . 12	
13	**PENALTY.** Subtract line 12 from line 11. Enter the result here and on Form 540, line 113; Long Form 540NR, line 123; or Form 541, line 44. Also, check the box for "FTB 5805." ▶ WAIVER $22.00 ◉ 13	0.

FILE COPY

Form 1040 Department of the Treasury - Internal Revenue Service (99) U.S. Individual Income Tax Return 2014

OMB No. 1545-0074 | IRS Use Only - Do not write or staple in this space.

For the year Jan. 1-Dec. 31, 2014, or other tax year beginning , ending | See separate instructions.

Your first name and initial	Last name	Your social security number
[redacted]	[redacted]	[redacted]
If a joint return, spouse's first name and initial	Last name	Spouse's social security number
Home address (number and street). If you have a P.O. box, see instructions.	Apt. no. [redacted]	Make sure the SSN(s) above and on line 6c are correct.
City, town or post office, state, and ZIP code. If you have a foreign address, also complete spaces below (see instructions). [redacted]		Presidential Election Campaign Check here if you, or your spouse if filing jointly, want $3 to go to this fund. Checking a box below will not change your tax or refund. ☐ You ☐ Spouse
Foreign country name	Foreign province/state/county	Foreign postal code

Filing Status

Check only one box.

1 [X] Single
2 ☐ Married filing jointly (even if only one had income)
3 ☐ Married filing separately. Enter spouse's SSN above and full name here. ▶
4 ☐ Head of household (with qualifying person). (See instructions.) If the qualifying person is a child but not your dependent, enter this child's name here. ▶
5 ☐ Qualifying widow(er) with dependent child

Exemptions

6a [X] **Yourself.** If someone can claim you as a dependent, **do not** check box 6a
b ☐ **Spouse**

Boxes checked on 6a and 6b: 1

c **Dependents:**

(1) First name Last name	(2) Dependent's social security number	(3) Dependent's relationship to you	(4) ✓ if child under age 17 qualifying for child tax credit (see instr.)
			☐
			☐
			☐
			☐

If more than four dependents, see instructions and check here ▶ ☐

No. of children on 6c who: • lived with you: 0
• did not live with you due to divorce or separation (see instructions): 0
Dependents on 6c not entered above: 0

d Total number of exemptions claimed — Add numbers on lines above ▶ 1

Income

Attach Form(s) W-2 here. Also attach Forms W-2G and 1099-R if tax was withheld.

If you did not get a W-2, see instructions.

Line	Description		Amount
7	Wages, salaries, tips, etc. Attach Form(s) W-2	7	56,146.
8a	**Taxable** interest. Attach Schedule B if required	8a	
b	**Tax-exempt** interest. **Do not** include on line 8a — 8b		
9a	Ordinary dividends. Attach Schedule B if required	9a	
b	Qualified dividends — 9b		
10	Taxable refunds, credits, or offsets of state and local income taxes	10	
11	Alimony received	11	
12	Business income or (loss). Attach Schedule C or C-EZ	12	67,524.
13	Capital gain or (loss). Attach Schedule D if required. If not required, check here ▶ ☐	13	
14	Other gains or (losses). Attach Form 4797	14	
15a	IRA distributions — 15a — b Taxable amount	15b	
16a	Pensions and annuities — 16a — b Taxable amount	16b	4.
17	Rental real estate, royalties, partnerships, S corporations, trusts, etc. Attach Schedule E	17	
18	Farm income or (loss). Attach Schedule F	18	
19	Unemployment compensation	19	
20a	Social security benefits — 20a — b Taxable amount	20b	
21	Other income. List type and amount See Attached	21	1,334.
22	Combine the amounts in the far right column for lines 7 through 21. This is your **total income** ▶	22	125,008.

Adjusted Gross Income

Line	Description		Amount		Amount
23	Educator expenses	23			
24	Certain business expenses of reservists, performing artists, and fee-basis government officials. Attach Form 2106 or 2106-EZ	24			
25	Health savings account deduction. Attach Form 8889	25			
26	Moving expenses. Attach Form 3903	26			
27	Deductible part of self-employment tax. Attach Schedule SE	27	4,674.		
28	Self-employed SEP, SIMPLE, and qualified plans	28			
29	Self-employed health insurance deduction	29	9,000.		
30	Penalty on early withdrawal of savings	30			
31a	Alimony paid b Recipient's SSN ▶	31a			
32	IRA deduction	32			
33	Student loan interest deduction	33			
34	Tuition and fees. Attach Form 8917	34			
35	Domestic production activities deduction. Attach Form 8903	35			
36	Add lines 23 through 35			36	13,674.
37	Subtract line 36 from line 22. This is your **adjusted gross income** ▶			37	111,334.

For Disclosure, Privacy Act, and Paperwork Reduction Act Notice, see separate instructions. Form 1040 (2014)

UYA

Tax and Credits

38	Amount from line 37 (adjusted gross income)	38	111,334.
39a	Check if: ☐ You were born before January 2, 1950, ☐ Blind. ☐ Spouse was born before January 2, 1950, ☐ Blind. Total boxes checked ▶ 39a 0		
b	If your spouse itemizes on a separate return or you were a dual-status alien, check here ▶ 39b ☐		
40	Itemized deductions (from Schedule A) or your standard deduction (see left margin)	40	6,200.
41	Subtract line 40 from line 38	41	105,134.
42	Exemptions. If line 38 is $152,525 or less, multiply $3,950 by the number on line 6d. Otherwise, see instructions	42	3,950.
43	Taxable income. Subtract line 42 from line 41. If line 42 is more than line 41, enter -0-	43	101,184.
44	Tax (see instructions). Check if any from: a ☐ Form(s) 8814 b ☐ Form 4972 c ☐	44	21,507.
45	Alternative minimum tax (see instructions). Attach Form 6251	45	
46	Excess advance premium tax credit repayment. Attach Form 8962	46	
47	Add lines 44, 45, and 46 ▶	47	21,507.
48	Foreign tax credit. Attach Form 1116 if required	48	
49	Credit for child and dependent care expenses. Attach Form 2441	49	
50	Education credits from Form 8863, line 19	50	
51	Retirement savings contributions credit. Attach Form 8880	51	
52	Child tax credit. Attach Schedule 8812, if required	52	
53	Residential energy credits. Attach Form 5695	53	
54	Other credits from Form: a ☐ 3800 b ☐ 8801 c ☐	54	
55	Add lines 48 through 54. These are your total credits	55	0.
56	Subtract line 55 from line 47. If line 55 is more than line 47, enter -0- ▶	56	21,507.

Standard Deduction for—
- People who check any box on line 39a or 39b or who can be claimed as a dependent, see instructions.
- All others: Single or Married filing separately, $6,200; Married filing jointly or Qualifying widow(er), $12,400; Head of household, $9,100

Other Taxes

57	Self-employment tax. Attach Schedule SE	57	9,347.
58	Unreported social security and Medicare tax from Form: a ☐ 4137 b ☐ 8919	58	
59	Additional tax on IRAs, other qualified retirement plans, etc. Attach Form 5329 if required	59	
60a	Household employment taxes from Schedule H	60a	
b	First-time homebuyer credit repayment. Attach Form 5405 if required	60b	
61	Health care: individual responsibility (see instructions) Full-year coverage ☒	61	
62	Taxes from: a ☐ Form 8959 b ☐ Form 8960 c ☐ Instructions; enter code(s)	62	
63	Add lines 56 through 62. This is your total tax ▶	63	30,854.

Payments

64	Federal income tax withheld from Forms W-2 and 1099	64	10,782.
65	2014 estimated tax payments and amount applied from 2013 return	65	
66a	Earned income credit (EIC) NO	66a	
b	Nontaxable combat pay election 66b		
67	Additional child tax credit. Attach Schedule 8812	67	
68	American opportunity credit from Form 8863, line 8	68	
69	Net premium tax credit. Attach Form 8962	69	
70	Amount paid with request for extension to file	70	
71	Excess social security and tier 1 RRTA tax withheld	71	
72	Credit for federal tax on fuels. Attach Form 4136	72	
73	Credits from Form: a ☐ 2439 b Reserved c Reserved d ☐	73	
74	Add lines 64, 65, 66a, and 67 through 73. These are your total payments ▶	74	10,782.

If you have a qualifying child, attach Schedule EIC.

Refund

75	If line 74 is more than line 63, subtract line 63 from line 74. This is the amount you overpaid	75	0.
76a	Amount of line 75 you want refunded to you. If Form 8888 is attached, check here ▶ ☐	76a	0.
▶ b	Routing number ▶ c Type: ☐ Checking ☐ Savings		
▶ d	Account number		
77	Amount of line 75 you want applied to your 2015 estimated tax ▶ 77		

Direct deposit? See instructions.

Amount You Owe

78	Amount you owe. Subtract line 74 from line 63. For details on how to pay, see instructions ▶	78	20,072.
79	Estimated tax penalty (see instructions) 79		

Third Party Designee

Do you want to allow another person to discuss this return with the IRS (see instructions)? ☐ Yes. Complete below. ☒ No

Designee's name ▶ Phone no. ▶ Personal identification number (PIN) ▶

Sign Here

Under penalties of perjury, I declare that I have examined this return and accompanying schedules and statements, and to the best of my knowledge and belief, they are true, correct, and complete. Declaration of preparer (other than taxpayer) is based on all information of which preparer has any knowledge.

Joint return? See instr. Keep a copy for your records.

Your signature	Date	Your occupation	Daytime phone number
		Travel Phy. Therap.	
Spouse's signature. If a joint return, both must sign.	Date	Spouse's occupation	If the IRS sent you an Identity Protection PIN, enter it here (see inst.)

Paid Preparer Use Only

Print/Type preparer's name	Preparer's signature	Date	Check ☒ if self-employed	PTIN
Lucina V de los Reyes	Lucina V. delosReyes	4/12/15		

Firm's name ▶ Lucina V de los Reyes — Firm's EIN ▶ 27-2432384

Firm's address ▶ 1529 Hampton Court, Naperville, IL 60565 — Phone no.

SCHEDULE C (Form 1040)

Department of the Treasury Internal Revenue Service (99)

Profit or Loss From Business

(Sole Proprietorship)

▶ Information about Schedule C and its separate instructions is at *www.irs.gov/schedulec.*
▶ Attach to Form 1040, 1040NR, or 1041; partnerships generally must file Form 1065.

OMB No. 1545-0074 **2014** Attachment Sequence No. **09**

Name of proprietor | Social security number (SSN)

A Principal business or profession, including product or service (see instructions)
Travelling Physical Therapist

B Enter code from instructions ▶

C Business name. If no separate business name, leave blank.

D Employer ID number (EIN), (see instr.)

E Business address (including suite or room no.) ▶
City, town or post office, state, and ZIP code

F Accounting method: (1) [X] Cash (2) [ ] Accrual (3) [ ] Other (specify) ▶

G Did you "materially participate" in the operation of this business during 2014? If "No," see instructions for limit on losses [X] Yes [ ] No

H If you started or acquired this business during 2014, check here ▶ [ ]

I Did you make any payments in 2014 that would require you to file Form(s) 1099? (see instructions) [ ] Yes [ ] No

J If "Yes," did you or will you file required Forms 1099? [ ] Yes [ ] No

Part I Income

1	Gross receipts or sales. See instructions for line 1 and check the box if this income was reported to you on Form W-2 and the "Statutory employee" box on that form was checked ▶ [ ]	1	129,324.
2	Returns and allowances	2	
3	Subtract line 2 from line 1	3	129,324.
4	Cost of goods sold (from line 42)	4	
5	**Gross profit.** Subtract line 4 from line 3	5	129,324.
6	Other income, including federal and state gasoline or fuel tax credit or refund (see instructions)	6	
7	**Gross income.** Add lines 5 and 6 ▶	7	129,324.

Part II Expenses. Enter expenses for business use of your home only on line 30.

8	Advertising	8	150.	18	Office expense (see instructions)	18	
9	Car and truck expenses (see instructions)	9	26,900.	19	Pension and profit-sharing plans	19	
				20	Rent or lease (see instructions):		
10	Commissions and fees	10		a	Vehicles, machinery, and equipment	20a	
11	Contract labor (see instructions)	11		b	Other business property	20b	
12	Depletion	12		21	Repairs and maintenance	21	4,000.
13	Depreciation and section 179 expense deduction (not included in Part III) (see instructions)	13		22	Supplies (not included in Part III)	22	2,000.
				23	Taxes and licenses	23	250.
				24	Travel, meals, and entertainment:		
14	Employee benefit programs (other than on line 19)	14		a	Travel	24a	14,400.
15	Insurance (other than health)	15	350.	b	Deductible meals and entertainment (see instructions)	24b	
16	Interest:			25	Utilities	25	
a	Mortgage (paid to banks, etc.)	16a		26	Wages (less employment credits)	26	
b	Other	16b		27a	Other expenses (from line 48)	27a	12,400.
17	Legal and professional services	17	350.	b	**Reserved for future use**	27b	

28	**Total expenses** before expenses for business use of home. Add lines 8 through 27a ▶	28	60,800.
29	Tentative profit or (loss). Subtract line 28 from line 7	29	68,524.
30	Expenses for business use of your home. Do not report these expenses elsewhere. Attach Form 8829 unless using the simplified method (see instructions). **Simplified method filers only:** enter the total square footage of: (a) your home: 1000 and (b) the part of your home used for business: 200. Use the Simplified Method Worksheet in the instructions to figure the amount to enter on line 30	30	1,000.
31	**Net profit or (loss).** Subtract line 30 from line 29. • If a profit, enter on both **Form 1040, line 12** (or **Form 1040NR, line 13**) and on **Schedule SE, line 2.** (If you checked the box on line 1, see instructions). Estates and trusts, enter on **Form 1041, line 3.** • If a loss, you **must** go to line 32.	31	67,524.

32 If you have a loss, check the box that describes your investment in this activity (see instructions).
• If you checked 32a, enter the loss on both Form 1040, line 12, (or Form 1040NR, line 13) and on **Schedule SE, line 2.** (If you checked the box on line 1, see the line 31 instructions). Estates and trusts, enter on Form 1041, line 3
• If you checked 32b, you **must** attach Form 6198. Your loss may be limited.

32a [ ] All investment is at risk.
32b [ ] Some investment is not at risk.

For Paperwork Reduction Act Notice, see the separate instructions. UYA **Schedule C (Form 1040) 2014**

Part III **Cost of Goods Sold** (see instructions)

33 Method(s) used to value closing inventory: a ☐ Cost b ☐ Lower of cost or market c ☐ Other (attach explanation)

34 Was there any change in determining quantities, costs, or valuations between opening and closing inventory? If "Yes," attach explanation . . . ☐ Yes ☐ No

35	Inventory at beginning of year. If different from last year's closing inventory, attach explanation	35	
36	Purchases less cost of items withdrawn for personal use	36	
37	Cost of labor. Do not include any amounts paid to yourself	37	
38	Materials and supplies	38	
39	Other costs	39	
40	Add lines 35 through 39	40	
41	Inventory at end of year	41	
42	**Cost of goods sold.** Subtract line 41 from line 40. Enter the result here and on line 4	42	0.

Part IV **Information on Your Vehicle.** Complete this part **only** if you are claiming car or truck expenses on line 9 and are not required to file Form 4562 for this business. See the instructions for line 13 to find out if you must file Form 4562.

43 When did you place your vehicle in service for business purposes? (month, day, year) ▶

44 Of the total number of miles you drove your vehicle during 2014, enter the number of miles you used your vehicle for:

a Business 0 b Commuting (see instructions) 0 c Other 0

45 Was your vehicle available for personal use during off-duty hours? . . . ☐ Yes ☐ No

46 Do you (or your spouse) have another vehicle available for personal use? . . . ☐ Yes ☐ No

47a Do you have evidence to support your deduction? . . . ☐ Yes ☐ No

b If "Yes," is the evidence written? . . . ☐ Yes ☐ No

Part V **Other Expenses.** List below business expenses not included on lines 8-26 or line 30.

Uniforms, PT tools	5,000.
Cellphone, Phone bills	2,700.
Internet	1,500.
Ipad	700.
Continuing education/seminars	2,500.
48 **Total other expenses.** Enter here and on line 27a . . . 48	12,400.

Name of person with self-employment income (as shown on Form 1040 or Form 1040NR) | Social security number of person with self-employment income ▶

Section B - Long Schedule SE

Part I Self-Employment Tax

Note. If your only income subject to self-employment tax is **church employee income,** see instructions. Also see instructions for the definition of church employee income.

A	If you are a minister, member of a religious order, or Christian Science practitioner and you filed Form 4361, but you had $400 or more of **other** net earnings from self-employment, check here and continue with Part I ▶ ☐		
1a	Net farm profit or (loss) from Schedule F, line 34 and farm partnerships, Schedule K-1 (Form 1065), box 14, code A. **Note.** Skip lines 1a and 1b if you use the farm optional method (see inst.)	1a	
b	If you received social security retirement or disability benefits, enter the amount of Conservation Reserve Program payments included on Schedule F, line 4b, or listed on Schedule K-1 (Form 1065), box 20, code Z	1b	( )
2	Net profit or (loss) from Schedule C, line 31; Schedule C-EZ, line 3; Schedule K-1 (Form 1065), box 14, code A (other than farming); and Schedule K-1 (Form 1065-B), box 9, code J1. Ministers and members of religious orders, see instructions for types of income to report on this line. See instructions for other income to report. **Note.** Skip this line if you use the nonfarm optional method (see instructions)	2	67,524.
3	Combine lines 1a, 1b, and 2	3	67,524.
4a	If line 3 is more than zero, multiply line 3 by 92.35% (.9235). Otherwise, enter amount from line 3. **Note.** If line 4a is less than $400 due to Conservation Reserve Program payments on line 1b, see instructions.	4a	62,358.
b	If you elect one or both of the optional methods, enter the total of lines 15 and 17 here	4b	
c	Combine lines 4a and 4b. If less than $400, **stop;** you do not owe self-employment tax. **Exception.** If less than $400 and you had **church employee income,** enter -0- and continue ▶	4c	62,358.
5a	Enter your **church employee income** from Form W-2. See instructions for definition of church employee income. 5a		
b	Multiply line 5a by 92.35% (.9235). If less than $100, enter -0-	5b	0.
6	Add lines 4c and 5b	6	62,358.
7	Maximum amount of combined wages and self-employment earnings subject to social security tax or the 6.2% portion of the 7.65% railroad retirement (tier 1) tax for 2014	7	117,000
8a	Total social security wages and tips (total of boxes 3 and 7 on Form(s) W-2) and railroad retirement (tier 1) compensation. If $117,000 or more, skip lines 8b through 10, and go to line 11 — 8a: 56,198.		
b	Unreported tips subject to social security tax (from Form 4137, line 10) — 8b		
c	Wages subject to social security tax (from Form 8919, line 10) — 8c		
d	Add lines 8a, 8b, and 8c	8d	56,198.
9	Subtract line 8d from line 7. If zero or less, enter -0- here and on line 10 and go to line 11 ▶	9	60,802.
10	Multiply the **smaller** of line 6 or line 9 by 12.4% (.124)	10	7,539.
11	Multiply line 6 by 2.9% (.029)	11	1,808.
12	**Self-employment tax.** Add lines 10 and 11. Enter here and on **Form 1040, line 57,** or **Form 1040NR, line 55**	12	9,347.
13	**Deduction for one-half of self-employment tax.** Multiply line 12 by 50% (.50). Enter the result here and on **Form 1040, line 27, or Form 1040NR, line 27** — 13: 4,674.		

Part II Optional Methods To Figure Net Earnings (see instructions)

Farm Optional Method. You may use this method **only** if (a) your gross farm income[1] was not more than $7,200 **or (b)** your net farm profits[2] were less than $5,198.

14	Maximum income for optional methods	14	4,800
15	Enter the **smaller** of: two-thirds (2/3) of gross farm income[1] (not less than zero) **or** $4,800. Also include this amount on line 4b above	15	

Nonfarm Optional Method. You may use this method only if (a) your net nonfarm profits[3] were less than $5,198 and also less than 72.189% of your gross nonfarm income,[4] and (b) you had net earnings from self-employment of at least $400 in 2 of the prior 3 years. **Caution.** You may use this method no more than five times.

16	Subtract line 15 from line 14	16	
17	Enter the **smaller** of: two-thirds (2/3) of gross nonfarm income[4] (not less than zero) **or** the amount on line 16. Also include this amount on line 4b above	17	

[1] From Sch. F, line 9, and Sch. K-1 (Form 1065), box 14, code B.

[2] From Sch. F, line 34, and Sch. K-1 (Form 1065), box 14, code A — minus the amount you would have entered on line 1b had you not used the optional method.

[3] From Sch. C, line 31; Sch. C-EZ, line 3; Sch. K-1 (Form 1065), box 14, code A; and Sch. K-1 (Form 1065-B), box 9, code J1.

[4] From Sch. C, line 7; Sch. C-EZ, line 1; Sch. K-1 (Form 1065), box 14, code C; and Sch. K-1 (Form 1065-B), box 9, code J2.

Form **4562** Department of the Treasury Internal Revenue Service (99)

Depreciation and Amortization (Including Information on Listed Property)

▶ Attach to your tax return.

▶ Information about Form 4562 and its separate instructions is at www.irs.gov/form4562

OMB No. 1545-0172 **2014** Attachment Sequence No. **179**

Name(s) shown on return	Business or activity to which this form relates	Identifying number
[redacted]	Travelling Physical Therapist	[redacted]

Part I Election To Expense Certain Property Under Section 179

Note: *If you have any listed property, complete Part V before you complete Part I.*

1	Maximum amount (see instructions)	1	
2	Total cost of section 179 property placed in service (see instructions)	2	
3	Threshold cost of section 179 property before reduction in limitation (see instructions)	3	
4	Reduction in limitation. Subtract line 3 from line 2. If zero or less, enter -0-	4	0.
5	Dollar limitation for tax year. Subtract line 4 from line 1. If zero or less, enter -0-. If married filing separately, see instructions	5	0.

6 (a) Description of property	(b) Cost (business use only)	(c) Elected cost

7	Listed property. Enter the amount from line 29	7	
8	Total elected cost of section 179 property. Add amounts in column (c), lines 6 and 7	8	
9	Tentative deduction. Enter the smaller of line 5 or line 8	9	
10	Carryover of disallowed deduction from line 13 of your 2013 Form 4562	10	
11	Business income limitation. Enter the smaller of business income (not less than zero) or line 5 (see instructions)	11	
12	Section 179 expense deduction. Add lines 9 and 10, but do not enter more than line 11	12	
13	Carryover of disallowed deduction to 2015. Add lines 9 and 10, less line 12 ▶	13	

Note: *Do not use Part II or Part III below for listed property. Instead, use Part V.*

Part II Special Depreciation Allowance and Other Depreciation (Do not include listed property.) (See instructions.)

14	Special depreciation allowance for qualified property (other than listed property) placed in service during the tax year (see instructions)	14	
15	Property subject to section 168(f)(1) election	15	
16	Other depreciation (including ACRS)	16	

Part III MACRS Depreciation (Do not include listed property.) (See instructions.)

Section A

17	MACRS deductions for assets placed in service in tax years beginning before 2014	17	
18	If you are electing to group any assets placed in service during the tax year into one or more general asset accounts, check here ▶ ☐		

Section B — Assets Placed in Service During 2014 Tax Year Using the General Depreciation System

(a) Classification of property	(b) Month and year placed in service	(c) Basis for depreciation (business/investment use only - see instructions)	(d) Recovery period	(e) Convention	(f) Method	(g) Depreciation deduction
19a 3-year property						
b 5-year property						
c 7-year property						
d 10-year property						
e 15-year property						
f 20-year property						
g 25-year property			25 yrs.		S/L	
h Residential rental property			27.5 yrs.	MM	S/L	
			27.5 yrs.	MM	S/L	
i Nonresidential real property			39 yrs.	MM	S/L	
				MM	S/L	

Section C — Assets Placed in Service During 2014 Tax Year Using the Alternative Depreciation System

(a)	(b)	(c)	(d)	(e)	(f)	(g)
20a Class life					S/L	
b 12-year			12 yrs.		S/L	
c 40-year			40 yrs.	MM	S/L	

Part IV Summary (See instructions)

21	Listed property. Enter amount from line 28	21	
22	**Total.** Add amounts from line 12, lines 14 through 17, lines 19 and 20 in column (g), and line 21. Enter here and on the appropriate lines of your return. Partnerships and S corporations - see instructions	22	0.
23	For assets shown above and placed in service during the current year, enter the portion of the basis attributable to section 263A costs	23	

Part V **Listed Property** (include automobiles, certain other vehicles, certain aircraft, certain computers, and property used for entertainment, recreation, or amusement.)

Note: *For any vehicle for which you are using the standard mileage rate or deducting lease expense, complete* ***only*** *24a, 24b, columns (a) through (c) of Section A, all of Section B, and Section C if applicable.*

Section A—Depreciation and Other Information (Caution: *See the instructions for limits for passenger automobiles.*)

24a Do you have evidence to support the business/investment use claimed? ☐ Yes ☐ No **24b** If "Yes," is the evidence written? ☐ Yes ☐ No

(a) Type of property (list vehicles first)	(b) Date placed in service	(c) Business/ investment use percentage	(d) Cost or other basis	(e) Basis for depreciation (business/investment use only)	(f) Recovery period	(g) Method/ Convention	(h) Depreciation deduction	(i) Elected section 179 cost
25 Special depreciation allowance for qualified listed property placed in service during the tax year and used more than 50% in a qualified business use (see instructions)						25		
26 Property used more than 50% in a qualified business use:								
Car	02/25/02	100.0%						
		%						
		%						
27 Property used 50% or less in a qualified business use:								
		%				S/L -		
		%				S/L -		
		%				S/L -		
28 Add amounts in column (h), lines 25 through 27. Enter here and on line 21, page 1						28		
29 Add amounts in column (i), line 26. Enter here and on line 7, page 1							29	

Section B—Information on Use of Vehicles

Complete this section for vehicles used by a sole proprietor, partner, or other "more than 5% owner," or related person. If you provided vehicles to your employees, first answer the questions in Section C to see if you meet an exception to completing this section for those vehicles.

	Car (a) Vehicle 1		(b) Vehicle 2		(c) Vehicle 3		(d) Vehicle 4		(e) Vehicle 5		(f) Vehicle 6	
30 Total business/investment miles driven during the year (**do not** include commuting miles)	45000											
31 Total commuting miles driven during the year												
32 Total other personal (noncommuting) miles driven												
33 Total miles driven during the year. Add lines 30 through 32	45000											
	Yes	No	Yes	No	Yes	No	Yes	No	Yes	No	Yes	No
34 Was the vehicle available for personal use during off-duty hours?	X											
35 Was the vehicle used primarily by a more than 5% owner or related person?	X											
36 Is another vehicle available for personal use?	X											

Section C—Questions for Employers Who Provide Vehicles for Use by Their Employees

Answer these questions to determine if you meet an exception to completing Section B for vehicles used by employees who **are not** more than 5% owners or related persons (see instructions).

	Yes	No
37 Do you maintain a written policy statement that prohibits all personal use of vehicles, including commuting, by your employees?		
38 Do you maintain a written policy statement that prohibits personal use of vehicles, except commuting, by your employees? See the instructions for vehicles used by corporate officers, directors, or 1% or more owners		
39 Do you treat all use of vehicles by employees as personal use?		
40 Do you provide more than five vehicles to your employees, obtain information from your employees about the use of the vehicles, and retain the information received?		
41 Do you meet the requirements concerning qualified automobile demonstration use? (See instructions.)		

Note: *If your answer to 37, 38, 39, 40, or 41 is "Yes," do not complete Section B for the covered vehicles.*

Part VI **Amortization**

(a) Description of costs	(b) Date amortization begins	(c) Amortizable amount	(d) Code section	(e) Amortization period or percentage	(f) Amortization for this year
42 Amortization of costs that begins during your 2014 tax year (see instructions):					
43 Amortization of costs that began before your 2014 tax year				43	
44 **Total.** Add amounts in column (f). See the instructions for where to report				44	

2014 Other Income - Supporting Details for Form 1040, Line 21

Name(s) shown on Form 1040	Your social security number
[redacted]	[redacted]

Enter sources of other income below:	Jose	Not Applicable
1.		
2.		
3. Gambling Winnings reported on Form W-2G	1,334.	
Other winnings where a Form W-2G not received		
4. Jury Pay		
5. Net Operating Loss carry forward from 2013		
6. Foreign earned income exclusion from Form 2555		
7. Other Income from Schedule K-1		
8. Income from personal property rental		
9. Child's income amount from Form 8814, line 12		
10. MSA Distributions, Form 8853		
11. Medicare Advantage MSA Distributions, Form 8853		
12. Long-term Care Distribution, Form 8853		
13. Form 1099-MISC, Boxes 3 and 8		
14. Alaska Permanent Fund dividends		
15. Coverdell ESA or Qualified Tuition Program		
16. Cancellation of a nonbusiness debt, Form 1099-C		
17. Cancellation of a business debt, Partnership Sch K-1		
18. HSA Distributions, Form 8889		
19. Reemployment trade adjustment assistance (RTAA)		
20. Recapture of prior year tuition and fees deduction		
21. Recapture of charitable contribution deduction of a fractional interest in tangible personal property		
22. Recapture of charitable contribution deduction if no exempt use		
23. Income from Foreign Corporation, Form 5471		
24. Hobby income		
25. Income or loss, Form 8621		
26. Loss on excess deferral distribution		
27. Disaster relief payments		
28. Medicaid waiver payments to care provider (NOTICE 2014-07)		
29. Credit adjustment from regular income, Form 6478 and Form 8864		
Total Other Income	1,334.	

FORM

2014 California Resident Income Tax Return

540

APE

ATTACH FEDERAL RETURN

14 PBA 621610

A

R

RP

FILE COPY

Filing Status

1 [X] Single

2 [ ] Married/RDP filing jointly. See inst.

4 [ ] Head of household (with qualifying person). See instructions.

5 [ ] Qualifying widow(er) with dependent child. Enter year spouse/RDP died.

3 [ ] Married/RDP filing separately. Enter spouse's/RDP's SSN or ITIN above and full name here

If your California filing status is different from your federal filing status, check the box here . . . . ● [ ]

6 If someone can claim you (or your spouse/RDP) as a dependent, check the box here. See instructions . . . . ● 6 [ ]

Exemptions

▶ For line 7, line 8, line 9, and line 10: Multiply the amount you enter in the box by the pre-printed dollar amount for that line. **Whole dollars only**

7 **Personal:** If you checked box 1, 3, or 4 above, enter 1 in the box. If you checked box 2 or 5, enter 2 in the box. If you checked the box on line 6, see instructions ● 7 [1] X $108 = ● $ 108.

8 **Blind:** If you (or your spouse/RDP) are visually impaired, enter 1; if both are visually impaired, enter 2 . . . . ● 8 [ ] X $108 = ● $

9 **Senior:** If you (or your spouse/RDP) are 65 or older, enter 1; if both are 65 or older, enter 2 . . . . ● 9 [ ] X $108 = ● $

10 **Dependents:** Do not include yourself or your spouse/RDP.

First name	Last name	Dependent's relationship to you

Total dependent exemptions . . . . ● 10 [ ] X $333 = ● $

11 **Exemption amount:** Add line 7 through line 10. Transfer this amount to line 32. . . . . ● 11 $ 108.

Your name: [redacted] Your SSN or ITIN: [redacted]

Taxable Income

Line	Description		Amount
12	State wages from your Form(s) W-2, box 16. . . . . ● 12	56,146.	
13	Enter federal adjusted gross income from Form 1040, line 37; 1040A, line 21; or 1040EZ, line 4 . . . . . ◉ 13		111,334.
14	California adjustments - subtractions. Enter the amount from Schedule CA (540), line 37, column B ● 14		1,334.
15	Subtract line 14 from line 13. If less than zero, enter the result in parentheses. See instructions 15		110,000.
16	California adjustments - additions. Enter the amount from Schedule CA (540), line 37, column C . . . . ● 16		
17	California adjusted gross income. Combine line 15 and line 16 . . . . ● 17		110,000.
18	Enter the larger of: Your California itemized deductions from Schedule CA (540), line 44; OR Your California standard deduction shown below for your filing status: • Single or Married/RDP filing separately . . . . $3,992 • Married/RDP filing jointly, Head of household, or Qualifying widow(er) . . $7,984 If the box on line 6 is checked, STOP. See instructions. . . . . ● 18		3,992.
19	Subtract line 18 from line 17. This is your **taxable income**. If less than zero, enter -0-. . . . . ◉ 19		106,008.

Tax

Line	Description	Amount
31	Tax. Check box if from: ☐ Tax Table ☒ Tax Rate Schedule ● ☐ FTB 3800 ● ☐ FTB 3803 ● 31	7,368.
32	Exemption credits. Enter the amount from line 11. If your federal AGI is more than $176,413, see instr. ◉ 32	108.
33	Subtract line 32 from line 31. If less than zero, enter -0- . . . . ◉ 33	7,260.
34	Tax. (see instructions) Check box if from: ● ☐ Schedule G-1 ● ☐ Form FTB 5870A . . . ● 34	
35	Add line 33 and line 34. . . . . ◉ 35	7,260.

Special Credits

Line	Description	Amount
40	Nonrefundable Child and Dependent Care Expenses Credit. See instructions . . . . ● 40	
43	Enter credit name ☐ code ● ☐ and amount . . . . . ● 43	
44	Enter credit name ☐ code ● ☐ and amount . . . . . ● 44	
45	To claim more than two credits, see instructions. Attach Schedule P (540) . . . . ● 45	
46	Nonrefundable renter's credit. See instructions . . . . ● 46	
47	Add line 40 and line 43 through line 46. These are your total credits . . . . ◉ 47	0.
48	Subtract line 47 from line 35. If less than zero, enter -0- . . . . ◉ 48	7,260.

Your name: CAPISTRANO Your SSN or ITIN: 318-94-4769

Section	Line	Description		Amount
Other Taxes	61	Alternative minimum tax. Attach Schedule P (540)	61	
	62	Mental Health Services Tax. See instructions	62	
	63	Other taxes and credit recapture. See instructions	63	
	64	Add line 48, line 61, line 62, and line 63. This is your total tax	64	7,260.
Payments	71	California income tax withheld. See instructions	71	3,453.
	72	2014 CA estimated tax and other payments. See instructions	72	
	73	Real estate and other withholding. See instructions	73	
	74	Excess SDI (or VPDI) withheld. See instructions	74	
	75	Add line 71, line 72, line 73, and line 74. These are your total payments. See instructions	75	3,453.
Overpaid Tax/ Tax Due	91	Overpaid tax. If line 75 is more than line 64, subtract line 64 from line 75	91	
	92	Amount of line 91 you want applied to your 2015 estimated tax	92	
	93	Overpaid tax available this year. Subtract line 92 from line 91	93	
	94	Tax due. If line 75 is less than line 64, subtract line 75 from line 64	94	3,807.

Your name: CAPISTRANO Your SSN or ITIN: 318-94-4769

Use Tax

95 Use Tax. **This is not a total line.** See instructions . . . . ● 95

Contributions

	Code	Amount
California Seniors Special Fund. See instructions	● 400	
Alzheimer's Disease/Related Disorders Fund	● 401	
Rare and Endangered Species Preservation Program	● 403	
California Breast Cancer Research Fund	● 405	
California Firefighters' Memorial Fund	● 406	
Emergency Food for Families Fund	● 407	
California Peace Officer Memorial Foundation Fund	● 408	
California Sea Otter Fund	● 410	
California Cancer Research Fund	● 413	
Child Victims of Human Trafficking Fund	● 419	
School Supplies for Homeless Children Fund	● 422	
State Parks Protection Fund/Parks Pass Purchase	● 423	
Protect Our Coast and Oceans Fund	● 424	
Keep Arts in Schools Fund	● 425	
American Red Cross, California Chapters Fund	● 426	
California Senior Legislature Fund	● 427	
Habitat for Humanity Fund	● 428	
California Sexual Violence Victim Services Fund	● 429	
110 Add code 400 through code 429. This is your total contribution	● 110	

Your name: [redacted] Your SSN or ITIN: [redacted]

Amount You Owe

111 **AMOUNT YOU OWE.** Add line 94, line 95, and line 110. See instructions. **Do not send cash.**
Mail to: **FRANCHISE TAX BOARD**
PO BOX 942867
SACRAMENTO CA 94267-0001 . . . . 111 | 3,807.
Pay online – Go to **ftb.ca.gov** for more information.

Interest and Penalties

112 Interest, late return penalties, and late payment penalties . . . . 112 |

113 Underpayment of estimated tax. Check the box: ☐ **FTB 5805 attached** ☐ **FTB 5805F attached** 113 |

114 Total amount due. See instructions. Enclose, but **do not** staple, any payment . . . . 114 | 3,807.

Refund and Direct Deposit

115 **REFUND OR NO AMOUNT DUE.** Subtract line 95 and line 110 from line 93. See instructions
Mail to: **FRANCHISE TAX BOARD**
PO BOX 942840
SACRAMENTO CA 94240-0001 . . . . 115 | 0.

Fill in the information to authorize direct deposit of your refund into one or two accounts. **Do not** attach a voided check or a deposit slip. See instructions
Have you verified the routing and account numbers? Use whole dollars only.
All or the following amount of my refund (line 115) is authorized for direct deposit into the account shown below:

Routing number | Type ☐ Checking ☐ Savings | Account number | 116 Direct deposit amount

The remaining amount of my refund (line 115) is authorized for direct deposit into the account shown below:

Routing number | Type ☐ Checking ☐ Savings | Account number | 117 Direct deposit amount

IMPORTANT: See the instructions to find out if you should attach a copy of your complete federal tax return.

Under penalties of perjury, I declare that I have examined this tax return, including accompanying schedules and statements, and to the best of my knowledge and belief, it is true, correct, and complete.

Your signature | Date | Spouse's/RDP's signature (if a joint tax return, both must sign)

Sign Here

It is unlawful to forge a spouse's/RDP's signature.

Joint tax return? (See instructions.)

Your email address (optional). Enter only one email address.

Daytime phone number (optional): 650-515-1208

Paid preparer's signature (declaration of preparer is based on all information of which preparer has any knowledge): Lucina V. Delos Reyes

Firm's name (or yours, if self-employed): LUCINA V DE LOS REYES

PTIN: P01204841

Firm's address: 1529 HAMPTON COURT NAPERVILLE, IL 60565

FEIN: 27-2432384

Do you want to allow another person to discuss this tax return with us? See instructions . . . . ☐ Yes ☒ No

Print Third Party Designee's Name | Telephone Number

TAXABLE YEAR

2014

Wage and Tax Statement

CALIFORNIA SCHEDULE

W-2

Important: Attach this form to the back of your Form 540, 540 2EZ, or Form 540NR (Long or Short).

Name(s) as shown on tax return | SSN or ITIN

Caution: If this form is filled out **do not** send your Form(s) W-2 to the Franchise Tax Board. If your Form(s) W-2 are from multiple states, **attach** copies showing California tax withheld to this schedule. If this schedule is blank, attach your Form(s) W-2 to the lower front of your tax return.

All fields must be completed. DO NOT ATTACH PAYMENT TO THIS SCHEDULE.

* Employee's Social Security Number, name, and address must be the same as the information on the Form(s) W-2.

W-2 Information	1st W-2	2nd W-2
a. Employee's social security number *		
b. Employer identification number (EIN)		
c. Employer's name	IMPAQ REHABILITATION	HARDEN HOME HEALTH
Address	178 DENSLOWE DRIVE	12900 FOSTER
City	SAN FRANCISCO	OVERLAND PARK
State	CA	KS
Zip Code	94132	66213
e. Employee's first, middle initial and last name*		
f. Address*		
City*		
State*		
Zip Code*		
1. Wages, tips, other compensation	728.	55,418.
2. Federal income tax withheld	52.	10,729.
3. Social security wages	780.	55,418.
4. Social security tax withheld	48.	3,436.
6. Medicare tax withheld	11.	804.
7. Social security tips		
8. Allocated tips (not included in box 1)		

W-2 Information	1st W-2		2nd W-2	
10. Dependent care benefits				
11. Nonqualified plans				
12. Codes and amounts	Codes	Amounts	Codes	Amounts
	D	52.		
13. Check the appropriate box for: Statutory employee, Retirement plan, or Third-party sick pay	☐ Statutory employee		☐ Statutory employee	
	☒ Retirement plan		☐ Retirement plan	
	☐ Third-party sick pay		☐ Third-party sick pay	
14. SDI, VPDI, or CA SDI (from box 14 or 19)	Type: CA SDI	Amount: 8.	Type: CA SDI	Amount: 554.
15. State and employer's State ID number	State: CA	Employer's state ID number: [redacted]	State: CA	Employer's state ID number: [redacted]
16. State wages, tips, etc.	728.		55,418.	
17. State income tax	4.		3,449.	

TAXABLE YEAR

2014 **California Adjustments - Residents**

SCHEDULE **CA (540)**

Important: Attach this schedule behind Form 540, Side 5 as a supporting California schedule.

Name(s) as shown on tax return [redacted] | SSN or ITIN [redacted]

Part I Income Adjustment Schedule

Section A - Income		A Federal Amounts (taxable amounts from your federal tax return)	B Subtractions See instructions	C Additions See instructions
7 Wages, salaries, tips, etc. See instructions before making an entry in column B or C	7	56,146.		
8 Taxable interest (b)	8(a)			
9 Ordinary dividends. See instructions. (b)	9(a)			
10 Taxable refunds, credits, offsets of state and local income taxes	10			
11 Alimony received	11			
12 Business income or (loss)	12	67,524.		
13 Capital gain or (loss). See instructions	13			
14 Other gains or (losses)	14			
15 IRA distributions. See instructions. (a)	15(b)			
16 Pensions and annuities. See instructions. (a)	16(b)	4.		
17 Rental real estate, royalties, partnerships, S corporations, trusts, etc.	17			
18 Farm income or (loss)	18			
19 Unemployment compensation	19			
20 Social security benefits (a)	20(b)			
21 Other income. a California lottery winnings; b Disaster loss carryover from FTB 3805V; c Federal NOL (Form 1040, line 21); d NOL carryover from FTB 3805V; e NOL from FTB 3805D, 3805Z, 3806, 3807, or 3809; f Other (describe):	21	1,334	a 1,334. b c d e f	a b c d e f
22 Total. Combine line 7 through line 21 in column A. Add line 7 through line 21f in column B and column C. Go to Section B	22	125,008.	1,334.	0.

Section B - Adjustments to Income		A	B	C
23 Educator expenses	23			
24 Certain business expenses of reservists, performing artists, and fee-basis government officials	24			
25 Health savings account deduction	25			
26 Moving expenses	26			
27 Deductible part of self-employment tax	27	4,674.		
28 Self-employed SEP, SIMPLE, and qualified plans	28			
29 Self-employed health insurance deduction	29	9,000.		
30 Penalty on early withdrawal of savings	30			
31a Alimony paid. (b) Recipient's: SSN ____ Last name ____	31a			
32 IRA deduction	32			
33 Student loan interest deduction	33			
34 Tuition and fees	34			
35 Domestic production activities deduction	35			
36 Add lines 23 through line 31a and line 32 through line 35 in columns A, B, and C. See instructions	36	13,674.	0.	0.
37 Total. Subtract line 36 from line 22 in columns A, B, and C. See instructions	37	111,334.	1,334.	0.

Part II Adjustments to Federal Itemized Deductions

38	Federal itemized deductions. Enter the amount from federal Schedule A (Form 1040), lines 4, 9, 15, 19, 20, 27, and 28.	38	5,349.
39	Enter total of federal Schedule A (Form 1040), line 5 (State Disability Insurance, and state and local income tax, or General Sales Tax) and line 8 (foreign income taxes only). See instructions	39	4,015.
40	Subtract line 39 from line 38	40	1,334.
41	Other adjustments including California lottery losses. See instructions. Specify	41	
42	Combine line 40 and line 41	42	1,334.

43 Is your federal AGI (Form 540, line 13) more than the amount shown below for your filing status?

Single or married/RDP filing separately . . . $176,413
Head of household . . . $264,623
Married/RDP filing jointly or qualifying widow(er) . . . $352,830

No. Transfer the amount on line 42 to line 43.
Yes. Complete the Itemized Deductions Worksheet in the instructions for Schedule CA (540), line 43 . . . 43 1,334.

44 Enter the larger of the amount on line 43 or your standard deduction listed below

Single or married/RDP filing separately. See instructions . . . $3,992
Married/RDP filing jointly, head of household, or qualifying widow(er) . . . $7,984

Transfer the amount on line 44 to Form 540, line 18 . . . 44 3,992.

Form **1040** Department of the Treasury - Internal Revenue Service (99) **U.S. Individual Income Tax Return** **2013** OMB No. 1545-0074 IRS Use Only—Do not write or staple in this space. FILE COPY

For the year Jan. 1-Dec. 31, 2013, or other tax year beginning , 2013, ending , 20 See separate instructions.

Your first name and initial	Last name	Your social security number
[redacted]	[redacted]	[redacted]
If a joint return, spouse's first name and initial	Last name	Spouse's social security number
Home address (number and street). If you have a P.O. box, see instructions. [redacted]	Apt. no. [redacted]	Make sure the SSN(s) above and on line 6c are correct.
City, town or post office, state, and ZIP code. If you have a foreign address, also complete spaces below (see instructions). [redacted]		**Presidential Election Campaign** Check here if you, or your spouse if filing jointly, want $3 to go to this fund. Checking a box below will not change your tax or refund. ☐ You ☐ Spouse
Foreign country name	Foreign province/county / Foreign postal code	

Filing Status

Check only one box.

1 ☐ Single
2 ☐ Married filing jointly (even if only one had income)
3 ☐ Married filing separately. Enter spouse's SSN above and full name here. ▶
4 ☒ Head of household (with qualifying person). (See instructions.) If the qualifying person is a child but not your dependent, enter this child's name here. ▶
5 ☐ Qualifying widow(er) with dependent child

Exemptions

6a ☒ **Yourself.** If someone can claim you as a dependent, **do not** check box 6a
b ☐ **Spouse**

Boxes checked on 6a and 6b: 1

c **Dependents:**

(1) First name Last name	(2) Dependent's social security number	(3) Dependent's relationship to you	(4) ✓ if child under age 17 qualifying for child tax credit (see instr.)
Lourdes P Capistrano	620-69-5892	Parent	☐
			☐
			☐
			☐

If more than four dependents, see instructions and check here ▶ ☐

No. of children on 6c who: • lived with you: 0
• did not live with you due to divorce or separation (see instructions): 0
Dependents on 6c not entered above: 1

d Total number of exemptions claimed — Add numbers on lines above ▶ 2

Income

Attach Form(s) W-2 here. Also attach Forms W-2G and 1099-R if tax was withheld.

If you did not get a W-2, see instructions.

Line	Description		Amount
7	Wages, salaries, tips, etc. Attach Form(s) W-2	7	52,722.
8a	**Taxable** interest. Attach Schedule B if required	8a	
b	**Tax-exempt** interest. **Do not** include on line 8a — 8b		
9a	Ordinary dividends. Attach Schedule B if required	9a	
b	Qualified dividends — 9b		
10	Taxable refunds, credits, or offsets of state and local income taxes	10	
11	Alimony received	11	
12	Business income or (loss). Attach Schedule C or C-EZ	12	56,633.
13	Capital gain or (loss). Attach Schedule D if required. If not required, check here ▶ ☐	13	
14	Other gains or (losses). Attach Form 4797	14	
15a	IRA distributions — 15a — b Taxable amount	15b	
16a	Pensions and annuities — 16a — b Taxable amount	16b	12,382.
17	Rental real estate, royalties, partnerships, S corporations, trusts, etc. Attach Schedule E	17	
18	Farm income or (loss). Attach Schedule F	18	
19	Unemployment compensation	19	
20a	Social security benefits — 20a — b Taxable amount	20b	
21	Other income. List type and amount See Attached	21	1,410.
22	Combine the amounts in the far right column for lines 7 through 21. This is your **total income** ▶	22	123,147.

Adjusted Gross Income

Line	Description		Amount		
23	Educator expenses	23			
24	Certain business expenses of reservists, performing artists, and fee-basis government officials. Attach Form 2106 or 2106-EZ	24			
25	Health savings account deduction. Attach Form 8889	25			
26	Moving expenses. Attach Form 3903	26			
27	Deductible part of self-employment tax. Attach Schedule SE	27	4,001.		
28	Self-employed SEP, SIMPLE, and qualified plans	28			
29	Self-employed health insurance deduction	29	7,200.		
30	Penalty on early withdrawal of savings	30			
31a	Alimony paid b Recipient's SSN ▶	31a			
32	IRA deduction	32			
33	Student loan interest deduction	33			
34	Tuition and fees. Attach Form 8917	34			
35	Domestic production activities deduction. Attach Form 8903	35			
36	Add lines 23 through 35			36	11,201.
37	Subtract line 36 from line 22. This is your **adjusted gross income** ▶			37	111,946.

Section	Line	Description		Amount
Tax and Credits	38	Amount from line 37 (adjusted gross income)	38	111,946.
	39a	Check if: ☐ You were born before January 2, 1949, ☐ Blind. ☐ Spouse was born before January 2, 1949, ☐ Blind. Total boxes checked ▶ 39a 0		
	b	If your spouse itemizes on a separate return or you were a dual-status alien, check here ▶ 39b ☐		
	40	**Itemized deductions** (from Schedule A) or your **standard deduction** (see left margin)	40	8,950.
	41	Subtract line 40 from line 38	41	102,996.
	42	**Exemptions.** If line 38 is $150,000 or less, multiply $3,900 by the number on line 6d. Otherwise, see instructions	42	7,800.
	43	**Taxable income.** Subtract line 42 from line 41. If line 42 is more than line 41, enter -0-	43	95,196.
	44	Tax (see instructions). Check if any from: a ☐ Form(s) 8814 b ☐ Form 4972 c ☐	44	18,296.
	45	**Alternative minimum tax** (see instructions). Attach Form 6251	45	
	46	Add lines 44 and 45 ▶	46	18,296.
	47	Foreign tax credit. Attach Form 1116 if required	47	
	48	Credit for child and dependent care expenses. Attach Form 2441	48	
	49	Education credits from Form 8863, line 19	49	
	50	Retirement savings contributions credit. Attach Form 8880	50	
	51	Child tax credit. Attach Schedule 8812, if required	51	
	52	Residential energy credits. Attach Form 5695	52	
	53	Other credits from Form: a ☐ 3800 b ☐ 8801 c ☐	53	
	54	Add lines 47 through 53. These are your **total credits**	54	0.
	55	Subtract line 54 from line 46. If line 54 is more than line 46, enter -0- ▶	55	18,296.
Other Taxes	56	Self-employment tax. Attach Schedule SE	56	8,002.
	57	Unreported social security and Medicare tax from Form: a ☐ 4137 b ☐ 8919	57	
	58	Additional tax on IRAs, other qualified retirement plans, etc. Attach Form 5329 if required . . NO.	58	1,238.
	59a	Household employment taxes from Schedule H	59a	
	b	First-time homebuyer credit repayment. Attach Form 5405 if required	59b	
	60	Taxes from: a ☐ Form 8959 b ☐ Form 8960 c ☐ Instructions; enter code(s)	60	
	61	Add lines 55 through 60. This is your **total tax** ▶	61	27,536.
Payments	62	Federal income tax withheld from Forms W-2 and 1099	62	10,887.
	63	2013 estimated tax payments and amount applied from 2012 return	63	
	64a	**Earned income credit (EIC)** . . . NO.	64a	
	b	Nontaxable combat pay election 64b		
	65	Additional child tax credit. Attach Schedule 8812	65	
	66	American opportunity credit from Form 8863, line 8	66	
	67	Reserved	67	
	68	Amount paid with request for extension to file	68	
	69	Excess social security and tier 1 RRTA tax withheld	69	
	70	Credit for federal tax on fuels. Attach Form 4136	70	
	71	Credits from Form: a ☐ 2439 b Reserved c ☐ 8885 d ☐	71	
	72	Add lines 62, 63, 64a, and 65 through 71. These are your **total payments** ▶	72	10,887.
Refund	73	If line 72 is more than line 61, subtract line 61 from line 72. This is the amount you **overpaid**	73	0.
	74a	Amount of line 73 you want **refunded to you.** If Form 8888 is attached, check here ▶ ☐	74a	0.
	▶ b	Routing number ▶ c Type: ☐ Checking ☐ Savings		
	▶ d	Account number		
	75	Amount of line 73 you want **applied to your 2014 estimated tax** ▶	75	
Amount You Owe	76	**Amount you owe.** Subtract line 72 from line 61. For details on how to pay, see instructions ▶	76	16,926.
	77	Estimated tax penalty (see instructions)	77	277.

Standard Deduction for— • People who check any box on line 39a or 39b or who can be claimed as a dependent, see instructions. • All others: Single or Married filing separately, $6,100 Married filing jointly or Qualifying widow(er), $12,200 Head of household, $8,950

If you have a qualifying child, attach Schedule EIC.

Direct deposit? See instructions.

Third Party Designee Do you want to allow another person to discuss this return with the IRS (see instructions)? ☐ Yes. Complete below. ☒ No

Designee's name ▶ Phone no. ▶ Personal identification number (PIN) ▶

Sign Here Under penalties of perjury, I declare that I have examined this return and accompanying schedules and statements, and to the best of my knowledge and belief, they are true, correct, and complete. Declaration of preparer (other than taxpayer) is based on all information of which preparer has any knowledge.

Joint return? See instr. Keep a copy for your records.

Your signature | Date | Your occupation: Travel Phy. Therap. | Daytime phone number

Spouse's signature. If a joint return, both must sign. | Date | Spouse's occupation | If the IRS sent you an Identity Protection PIN, enter it here (see inst.)

Paid Preparer Use Only

Print/Type preparer's name: Lucina V de los Reyes | Preparer's signature: Lucina V. de los Reyes | Date: 4/15/14 | Check ☒ if self-employed | PTIN: P01204841

Firm's name ▶ Lucina V de los Reyes | Firm's EIN ▶ 27-2432384

Firm's address ▶ 1529 Hampton Court, Naperville, IL 60565 | Phone no.

SCHEDULE C (Form 1040)

Department of the Treasury Internal Revenue Service (99)

Profit or Loss From Business

(Sole Proprietorship)

▶ For information on Schedule C and its instructions, go to www.irs.gov/schedulec.
▶ Attach to Form 1040, 1040NR, or 1041; partnerships generally must file Form 1065.

OMB No. 1545-0074

2013

Attachment Sequence No. 09

Name of proprietor | Social security number (SSN)

A Principal business or profession, including product or service (see instructions)
Travelling Physical Therapist

B Enter code from instructions ▶

C Business name. If no separate business name, leave blank.

D Employer ID number (EIN), (see instr.)

E Business address (including suite or room no.) ▶
City, town or post office, state, and ZIP code

F Accounting method: (1) [X] Cash (2) [ ] Accrual (3) [ ] Other (specify) ▶

G Did you "materially participate" in the operation of this business during 2013? If "No," see instructions for limit on losses [X] Yes [ ] No

H If you started or acquired this business during 2013, check here ▶ [ ]

I Did you make any payments in 2013 that would require you to file Form(s) 1099? (see instructions) [ ] Yes [ ] No

J If "Yes," did you or will you file required Forms 1099? [ ] Yes [ ] No

Part I Income

1	Gross receipts or sales. See instructions for line 1 and check the box if this income was reported to you on Form W-2 and the "Statutory employee" box on that form was checked ▶ [ ]	1	104,695.
2	Returns and allowances	2	
3	Subtract line 2 from line 1	3	104,695.
4	Cost of goods sold (from line 42)	4	
5	**Gross profit.** Subtract line 4 from line 3	5	104,695.
6	Other income, including federal and state gasoline or fuel tax credit or refund (see instructions)	6	
7	**Gross income.** Add lines 5 and 6 ▶	7	104,695.

Part II Expenses

Enter expenses for business use of your home only on line 30.

8	Advertising	8	150.	18	Office expense (see instructions)	18	
9	Car and truck expenses (see instructions)	9	22,272.	19	Pension and profit-sharing plans	19	
				20	Rent or lease (see instructions):		
10	Commissions and fees	10			a Vehicles, machinery, and equipment	20a	
11	Contract labor (see instructions)	11			b Other business property	20b	
12	Depletion	12		21	Repairs and maintenance	21	3,500.
13	Depreciation and section 179 expense deduction (not included in Part III) (see instructions)	13		22	Supplies (not included in Part III)	22	850.
				23	Taxes and licenses	23	250.
				24	Travel, meals, and entertainment:		
14	Employee benefit programs (other than on line 19)	14			a Travel	24a	12,600.
15	Insurance (other than health)	15			b Deductible meals and entertainment (see instructions)	24b	
16	Interest:			25	Utilities	25	
a	Mortgage (paid to banks, etc.)	16a		26	Wages (less employment credits)	26	
b	Other	16b		27a	Other expenses (from line 48)	27a	7,990.
17	Legal and professional services	17	450.		b Reserved for future use	27b	

28	**Total expenses** before expenses for business use of home. Add lines 8 through 27a ▶	28	48,062.
29	Tentative profit or (loss). Subtract line 28 from line 7	29	56,633.
30	Expenses for business use of your home. Do not report these expenses elsewhere. Attach Form 8829 unless using the simplified method (see instructions). **Simplified method filers only:** enter the total square footage of: (a) your home: ____ and (b) the part of your home used for business: ____. Use the Simplified Method Worksheet in the instructions to figure the amount to enter on line 30	30	
31	**Net profit or (loss).** Subtract line 30 from line 29. • If a profit, enter on both **Form 1040, line 12** (or Form 1040NR, line 13) and on **Schedule SE, line 2**. (If you checked the box on line 1, see instructions). Estates and trusts, enter on **Form 1041, line 3.** • If a loss, you **must** go to line 32.	31	56,633.
32	If you have a loss, check the box that describes your investment in this activity (see instructions). • If you checked 32a, enter the loss on both **Form 1040, line 12,** (or **Form 1040NR, line 13**) and on **Schedule SE, line 2.** (If you checked the box on line 1, see the line 31 instructions). Estates and trusts, enter on **Form 1041, line 3** • If you checked 32b, you **must** attach **Form 6198**. Your loss may be limited.	32a [ ] All investment is at risk. 32b [ ] Some investment is not at risk.	

For Paperwork Reduction Act Notice, see the separate instructions. Schedule C (Form 1040) 2013

UYA

Part III **Cost of Goods Sold** (see instructions)

33 Method(s) used to value closing inventory: a ☐ Cost b ☐ Lower of cost or market c ☐ Other (attach explanation)

34 Was there any change in determining quantities, costs, or valuations between opening and closing inventory? If "Yes," attach explanation . . . ☐ Yes ☐ No

35	Inventory at beginning of year. If different from last year's closing inventory, attach explanation	35	
36	Purchases less cost of items withdrawn for personal use	36	
37	Cost of labor. Do not include any amounts paid to yourself	37	
38	Materials and supplies	38	
39	Other costs	39	
40	Add lines 35 through 39	40	
41	Inventory at end of year	41	
42	Cost of goods sold. Subtract line 41 from line 40. Enter the result here and on line 4	42	0.

Part IV **Information on Your Vehicle.** Complete this part **only** if you are claiming car or truck expenses on line 9 and are not required to file Form 4562 for this business. See the instructions for line 13 to find out if you must file Form 4562.

43 When did you place your vehicle in service for business purposes? (month, day, year) ▶

44 Of the total number of miles you drove your vehicle during 2013, enter the number of miles you used your vehicle for:

a Business 0 b Commuting (see instructions) 0 c Other 0

45 Was your vehicle available for personal use during off-duty hours? . . . ☐ Yes ☐ No

46 Do you (or your spouse) have another vehicle available for personal use? . . . ☐ Yes ☐ No

47a Do you have evidence to support your deduction? . . . ☐ Yes ☐ No

b If "Yes," is the evidence written? . . . ☐ Yes ☐ No

Part V **Other Expenses.** List below business expenses not included on lines 8-26 or line 30.

Uniforms, PT tools	3,500.
Cellphone	1,440.
Ipad, Computer,Fax machine	1,700.
Internet	1,350.
48 Total other expenses. Enter here and on line 27a (48)	7,990.

SCHEDULE SE (Form 1040)

Department of the Treasury Internal Revenue Service (99)

Self-Employment Tax

▶ Information about Schedule SE and its separate instructions is at www.irs.gov/schedulese.

▶ Attach to Form 1040 or Form 1040NR.

OMB No. 1545-0074

2013

Attachment Sequence No. **17**

Name of person with self-employment income (as shown on Form 1040)	Social security number of person with self-employment income ▶
[redacted]	[redacted]

Before you begin: To determine if you must file Schedule SE, see the instructions.

May I Use Short Schedule SE or Must I Use Long Schedule SE?

Note. Use this flowchart **only if** you must file Schedule SE. If unsure, see *Who Must File Schedule SE* in the instructions.

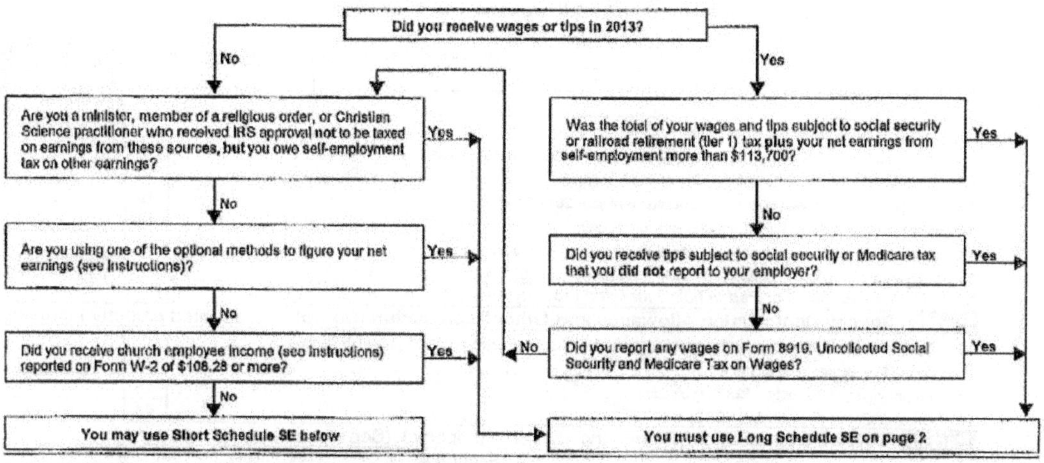

Section A - Short Schedule SE. Caution. Read above to see if you can use Short Schedule SE.

1a	Net farm profit or (loss) from Schedule F, line 34, and farm partnerships, Schedule K-1 (Form 1065), box 14, code A		**1a**	
b	If you received social security retirement or disability benefits, enter the amount of Conservation Reserve Program payments included on Schedule F, line 4b, or listed on Schedule K-1 (Form 1065), box 20, code Z		**1b**	( )
2	Net profit or (loss) from Schedule C, line 31; Schedule C-EZ, line 3; Schedule K-1 (Form 1065), box 14, code A (other than farming); and Schedule K-1 (Form 1065-B), box 9, code J1. Ministers and members of religious orders, see instructions for types of income to report on this line. See instructions for other income to report		**2**	56,633.
3	Combine lines 1a, 1b, and 2		**3**	56,633.
4	Multiply line 3 by 92.35% (.9235). If less than $400, you do not owe self-employment tax; **do not** file this schedule unless you have an amount on line 1b ▶ **Note.** If line 4 is less than $400 due to Conservation Reserve Program payments on line 1b, see instructions.		**4**	52,301.
5	**Self-employment tax.** If the amount on line 4 is: • $113,700 or less, multiply line 4 by 15.3% (.153). Enter the result here and on **Form 1040, line 56,** or **Form 1040NR, line 54** • More than $113,700, multiply line 4 by 2.9% (.029). Then, add $14,098.80 to the result. Enter the total here and on **Form 1040, line 56,** or **Form 1040NR, line 54**		**5**	8,002.
6	**Deduction for one-half of self-employment tax.** Multiply line 5 by 50% (.50). Enter the result here and on **Form 1040, line 27,** or **Form 1040NR, line 27**	**6** 4,001.		

For Paperwork Reduction Act Notice, see your tax return instructions.

UYA

Schedule SE (Form 1040) 2013

Form **4562** Department of the Treasury Internal Revenue Service (99)

Depreciation and Amortization
(Including Information on Listed Property)

▶ See separate instructions. ▶ Attach to your tax return.

OMB No. 1545-0172

2013 Attachment Sequence No. **179**

Name(s) shown on return	Business or activity to which this form relates	Identifying number
[redacted]	Travelling Physical Therapist	[redacted]

Part I Election To Expense Certain Property Under Section 179
Note: *If you have any listed property, complete Part V before you complete Part I.*

1	Maximum amount (see instructions)	1	
2	Total cost of section 179 property placed in service (see instructions)	2	
3	Threshold cost of section 179 property before reduction in limitation (see instructions)	3	
4	Reduction in limitation. Subtract line 3 from line 2. If zero or less, enter -0-	4	0.
5	Dollar limitation for tax year. Subtract line 4 from line 1. If zero or less, enter -0-. If married filing separately, see instructions	5	0.

6 (a) Description of property	(b) Cost (business use only)	(c) Elected cost

7	Listed property. Enter the amount from line 29	7	
8	Total elected cost of section 179 property. Add amounts in column (c), lines 6 and 7	8	
9	Tentative deduction. Enter the **smaller** of line 5 or line 8	9	
10	Carryover of disallowed deduction from line 13 of your 2012 Form 4562	10	
11	Business income limitation. Enter the smaller of business income (not less than zero) or line 5 (see instructions)	11	
12	Section 179 expense deduction. Add lines 9 and 10, but do not enter more than line 11	12	
13	Carryover of disallowed deduction to 2014. Add lines 9 and 10, less line 12 ▶	13	

Note: *Do not use Part II or Part III below for listed property. Instead, use Part V.*

Part II Special Depreciation Allowance and Other Depreciation (Do not include listed property.) (See instructions.)

14	Special depreciation allowance for qualified property (other than listed property) placed in service during the tax year (see instructions)	14	
15	Property subject to section 168(f)(1) election	15	
16	Other depreciation (including ACRS)	16	

Part III MACRS Depreciation (Do not include listed property.) (See instructions.)

Section A

17	MACRS deductions for assets placed in service in tax years beginning before 2013	17	
18	If you are electing to group any assets placed in service during the tax year into one or more general asset accounts, check here ▶ ☐		

Section B — Assets Placed in Service During 2013 Tax Year Using the General Depreciation System

(a) Classification of property	(b) Month and year placed in service	(c) Basis for depreciation (business/investment use only - see instructions)	(d) Recovery period	(e) Convention	(f) Method	(g) Depreciation deduction
19a 3-year property						
b 5-year property						
c 7-year property						
d 10-year property						
e 15-year property						
f 20-year property						
g 25-year property			25 yrs.		S/L	
h Residential rental property			27.5 yrs.	MM	S/L	
			27.5 yrs.	MM	S/L	
i Nonresidential real property			39 yrs.	MM	S/L	
				MM	S/L	

Section C — Assets Placed in Service During 2013 Tax Year Using the Alternative Depreciation System

20a Class life					S/L	
b 12-year			12 yrs.		S/L	
c 40-year			40 yrs.	MM	S/L	

Part IV Summary (See instructions)

21	Listed property. Enter amount from line 28	21	
22	**Total.** Add amounts from line 12, lines 14 through 17, lines 19 and 20 in column (g), and line 21. Enter here and on the appropriate lines of your return. Partnerships and S corporations - see instructions	22	0.
23	For assets shown above and placed in service during the current year, enter the portion of the basis attributable to section 263A costs	23	

For Paperwork Reduction Act Notice, see separate instructions.
UYA

Form **4562** (2013)

Part V **Listed Property** (Include automobiles, certain other vehicles, certain computers, and property used for entertainment, recreation, or amusement.)

Note: *For any vehicle for which you are using the standard mileage rate or deducting lease expense, complete* **only** *24a, 24b, columns (a) through (c) of Section A, all of Section B, and Section C if applicable.*

Section A — Depreciation and Other Information (Caution: *See the instructions for limits for passenger automobiles.*)

24a Do you have evidence to support the business/investment use claimed? ☐ Yes ☐ No **24b** If "Yes," is the evidence written? ☐ Yes ☐ No

(a) Type of property (list vehicles first)	(b) Date placed in service	(c) Business/ investment use percentage	(d) Cost or other basis	(e) Basis for depreciation (business/investment use only)	(f) Recovery period	(g) Method/ Convention	(h) Depreciation deduction	(i) Elected section 179 cost
25 Special depreciation allowance for qualified listed property placed in service during the tax year and used more than 50% in a qualified business use (see instructions) . . .						25		
26 Property used more than 50% in a qualified business use:								
Car	02/25/02	100.0 %						
		%						
		%						
27 Property used 50% or less in a qualified business use:								
		%				S/L -		
		%				S/L -		
		%				S/L -		
28 Add amounts in column (h), lines 25 through 27. Enter here and on line 21, page 1 . . .						28		
29 Add amounts in column (i), line 26. Enter here and on line 7, page 1 . . .							29	

Section B — Information on Use of Vehicles

Complete this section for vehicles used by a sole proprietor, partner, or other "more than 5% owner," or related person. If you provided vehicles to your employees, first answer the questions in Section C to see if you meet an exception to completing this section for those vehicles.

	Car (a) Vehicle 1		(b) Vehicle 2		(c) Vehicle 3		(d) Vehicle 4		(e) Vehicle 5		(f) Vehicle 6	
30 Total business/investment miles driven during the year (**do not** include commuting miles) .	37650											
31 Total commuting miles driven during the year												
32 Total other personal (noncommuting) miles driven . . .												
33 Total miles driven during the year. Add lines 30 through 32 . . .	37650											
	Yes	No	Yes	No	Yes	No	Yes	No	Yes	No	Yes	No
34 Was the vehicle available for personal use during off-duty hours? . . .	X											
35 Was the vehicle used primarily by a more than 5% owner or related person? . . .	X											
36 Is another vehicle available for personal use?	X											

Section C — Questions for Employers Who Provide Vehicles for Use by Their Employees

Answer these questions to determine if you meet an exception to completing Section B for vehicles used by employees who are **not** more than 5% owners or related persons (see instructions).

	Yes	No
37 Do you maintain a written policy statement that prohibits all personal use of vehicles, including commuting, by your employees? . . .		
38 Do you maintain a written policy statement that prohibits personal use of vehicles, except commuting, by your employees? See the instructions for vehicles used by corporate officers, directors, or 1% or more owners . . .		
39 Do you treat all use of vehicles by employees as personal use? . . .		
40 Do you provide more than five vehicles to your employees, obtain information from your employees about the use of the vehicles, and retain the information received? . . .		
41 Do you meet the requirements concerning qualified automobile demonstration use? (See instructions.) . . .		

Note: *If your answer to 37, 38, 39, 40, or 41 is "Yes," do not complete Section B for the covered vehicles.*

Part VI **Amortization**

(a) Description of costs	(b) Date amortization begins	(c) Amortizable amount	(d) Code section	(e) Amortization period or percentage	(f) Amortization for this year
42 Amortization of costs that begins during your 2013 tax year (see instructions):					
43 Amortization of costs that began before your 2013 tax year . . .				43	
44 **Total.** Add amounts in column (f). See the instructions for where to report . . .				44	

2013 Other Income - Supporting Details for Form 1040, Line 21

Name(s) shown on Form 1040	Your social security number
[redacted]	[redacted]

	Enter sources of other income below:	Jose	Not Applicab
1.			
2.			
3.	Gambling Winnings reported on Form W-2G	1,410.	
	Other winnings where a Form W-2G not received		
4.	Jury Pay		
5.	Net Operating Loss carry forward from 2012		
6.	Foreign earned income exclusion from Form 2555		
7.	Other Income from Schedule K-1		
8.	Income from personal property rental		
9.	Child's income amount from Form 8814, line 12		
10.	MSA Distributions, Form 8853		
11.	Medicare Advantage MSA Distributions, Form 8853		
12.	Long-term Care Distribution, Form 8853		
13.	Form 1099-MISC, Boxes 3 and 8		
14.	Alaska Permanent Fund dividends		
15.	Coverdell ESA or Qualified Tuition Program		
16.	Cancellation of a nonbusiness debt, Form 1099-C		
17.	Cancellation of a business debt, Partnership Sch K-1		
18.	HSA Distributions, Form 8889		
19.	Reemployment trade adjustment assistance (RTAA)		
20.	Recapture of prior year tuition and fees deduction		
21.	Recapture of charitable contribution deduction of a fractional interest in tangible personal property		
22.	Recapture of charitable contribution deduction if no exempt use		
23.	From 8891:		
24.	Income from Foreign Corporation, Form 5471		
25.	Hobby income		
26.	Income or loss, Form 8621		
27.	Loss on excess deferral distribution		
28.	Disaster relief payments		
	Total Other Income	1,410.	

For Privacy Notice, get FTB 1131 ENG/SP.

FORM

California Resident Income Tax Return 2013

540 C1 **Side 1**

APE

ATTACH FEDERAL RETURN

13 PBA 621610

A
R
RP

117 08-06-1971 FILE COPY

Filing Status

1 ☐ Single

2 ☐ Married/RDP filing jointly. See inst.

3 ☐ Married/RDP filing separately. Enter spouse's/RDP's SSN or ITIN above and full name here

4 ☒ Head of household (with qualifying person). See instructions.

5 ☐ Qualifying widow(er) with dependent child. Enter year spouse/RDP died.

If your California filing status is different from your federal filing status, check the box here ☐

6 If someone can claim you (or your spouse/RDP) as a dependent, check the box here. See instructions 6 ☐

Exemptions

▶ For line 7, line 8, line 9, and line 10: Multiply the amount you enter in the box by the pre-printed dollar amount for that line. **Whole dollars only**

7 **Personal:** If you checked box 1, 3, or 4 above, enter 1 in the box. If you checked box 2 or 5, enter 2 in the box. If you checked the box on line 6, see instructions 7 [1] X $106 = $ 106.

8 **Blind:** If you (or your spouse/RDP) are visually impaired, enter 1; if both are visually impaired, enter 2 8 [ ] X $106 = $

9 **Senior:** If you (or your spouse/RDP) are 65 or older, enter 1; If both are 65 or older, enter 2 9 [ ] X $106 = $

10 **Dependents: Do not include yourself or your spouse/RDP.**

First name	Last name	Dependent's relationship to you

Total dependent exemptions 10 [1] X $326 = $ 326.

11 **Exemption amount:** Add line 7 through line 10. Transfer this amount to line 32. 11 $ 432.

Your name: [redacted] Your SSN or ITIN: [redacted]

Section	Line	Description	Line ref	Amount
Taxable Income	12	State wages from your Form(s) W-2, box 16	12	52,721.
	13	Enter federal adjusted gross income from Form 1040, line 37; Form 1040A, line 21; or Form 1040EZ, line 4	13	111,946.
	14	California adjustments - subtractions. Enter the amount from Schedule CA (540), line 37, column B	14	
	15	Subtract line 14 from line 13. If less than zero, enter the result in parentheses. See instructions	15	111,946.
	16	California adjustments - additions. Enter the amount from Schedule CA (540), line 37, column C	16	
	17	California adjusted gross income. Combine line 15 and line 16	17	111,946.
	18	Enter the larger of: Your California **itemized deductions** from Schedule CA (540), line 44; OR Your California **standard deduction** shown below for your filing status: • Single or Married/RDP filing separately . . . $3,906 • Married/RDP filing jointly, Head of household, or Qualifying widow(er) . . $7,812. If the box on line 6 is checked, STOP. See instructions	18	7,812.
	19	Subtract line 18 from line 17. This is your **taxable income**. If less than zero, enter -0-	19	104,134.
Tax	31	Tax. Check box if from: ☐ Tax Table ☒ Tax Rate Schedule ☐ FTB 3800 ☐ FTB 3803	31	5,859.
	32	Exemption credits. Enter the amount from line 11. If your federal AGI is more than $172,615, see instr.	32	432.
	33	Subtract line 32 from line 31. If less than zero, enter -0-	33	5,427.
	34	Tax. (see instructions) Check box if from: ☐ Schedule G-1 ☐ Form FTB 5870A	34	
	35	Add line 33 and line 34	35	5,427.
Special Credits	40	Nonrefundable Child and Dependent Care Expenses Credit. See instructions	40	
	41	New jobs credit, amount generated. See instructions	41	
	42	New jobs credit, amount claimed. See instructions	42	
	43	Enter credit name ____ code ____ and amount	43	
	44	Enter credit name ____ code ____ and amount	44	
	45	To claim more than two credits, see instructions. Attach Schedule P (540)	45	
	46	Nonrefundable renter's credit. See instructions	46	
	47	Add line 40 and line 42 through line 46. These are your total credits	47	0.
	48	Subtract line 47 from line 35. If less than zero, enter -0-	48	5,427.

Your name: [redacted] Your SSN or ITIN: [redacted]

Other Taxes	61	Alternative minimum tax. Attach Schedule P (540)	• 61	
	62	Mental Health Services Tax. See instructions	• 62	
	63	Other taxes and credit recapture. See instructions 3805P.	• 63	310.
	64	Add line 48, line 61, line 62, and line 63. This is your total tax	• 64	5,737.
Payments	71	California income tax withheld. See instructions	• 71	3,347.
	72	2013 CA estimated tax and other payments. See instructions	• 72	
	73	Real estate and other withholding. See instructions	• 73	
	74	Excess SDI (or VPDI) withheld. See instructions	• 74	
	75	Add line 71, line 72, line 73, and line 74. These are your total payments. See instructions	⦿ 75	3,347.
Overpaid Tax/ Tax Due	91	Overpaid tax. If line 75 is more than line 64, subtract line 64 from line 75	⦿ 91	
	92	Amount of line 91 you want applied to your 2014 estimated tax	• 92	
	93	Overpaid tax available this year. Subtract line 92 from line 91	• 93	
	94	Tax due. If line 75 is less than line 64, subtract line 75 from line 64	⦿ 94	2,390.

Your name: [redacted] Your SSN or ITIN: [redacted]

Use Tax 95 Use Tax. This is not a total line. See instructions . . . . • 95

CONTRIBUTIONS

	Code	Amount
California Seniors Special Fund. See instructions	• 400	
Alzheimer's Disease/Related Disorders Fund	• 401	
California Fund for Senior Citizens	• 402	
Rare and Endangered Species Preservation Program	• 403	
State Children's Trust Fund for the Prevention of Child Abuse	• 404	
California Breast Cancer Research Fund	• 405	
California Firefighters' Memorial Fund	• 406	
Emergency Food for Families Fund	• 407	
California Peace Officer Memorial Foundation Fund	• 408	
California Sea Otter Fund	• 410	
Municipal Shelter Spay-Neuter Fund	• 412	
California Cancer Research Fund	• 413	
Child Victims of Human Trafficking Fund	• 419	
California YMCA Youth and Government Fund	• 420	
California Youth Leadership Fund	• 421	
School Supplies for Homeless Children Fund	• 422	
State Parks Protection Fund/Parks Pass Purchase	• 423	
Protect Our Coast and Oceans Fund	• 424	
Keep Arts in Schools Fund	• 425	
American Red Cross, California Chapters Fund	• 426	
110 Add code 400 through code 426. This is your total contribution	• 110	

Your name: [redacted] Your SSN or ITIN: [redacted]

Amount You Owe	111	AMOUNT YOU OWE. Add line 94, line 95, and line 110. See instructions. Do not send cash. Mail to: FRANCHISE TAX BOARD PO BOX 942867 SACRAMENTO CA 94267-0009. Pay online – Go to ftb.ca.gov for more information.	• 111	2,390.
Interest and Penalties	112	Interest, late return penalties, and late payment penalties	112	
	113	Underpayment of estimated tax. Check the box: • [X] FTB 5805 attached • [ ] FTB 5805F attached	• 113	33.
	114	Total amount due. See instructions. Enclose, but do not staple, any payment	114	2,423.
Refund and Direct Deposit	115	REFUND OR NO AMOUNT DUE. Subtract line 95 and line 110 from line 93. See instructions Mail to: FRANCHISE TAX BOARD PO BOX 942840 SACRAMENTO CA 94240-0009	• 115	0.

Fill in the information to authorize direct deposit of your refund into one or two accounts. Do not attach a voided check or a deposit slip. See instructions

Have you verified the routing and account numbers? Use whole dollars only.

All or the following amount of my refund (line 115) is authorized for direct deposit into the account shown below:

• Routing number | • Type [ ] Checking [ ] Savings | • Account number | • 116 Direct deposit amount

The remaining amount of my refund (line 115) is authorized for direct deposit into the account shown below:

• Routing number | • Type [ ] Checking [ ] Savings | • Account number | • 117 Direct deposit amount

IMPORTANT: See the instructions to find out if you should attach a copy of your complete federal tax return.

Under penalties of perjury, I declare that I have examined this tax return, including accompanying schedules and statements, and to the best of my knowledge and belief, it is true, correct, and complete.

Your signature | Date | Spouse's/RDP's signature (if a joint tax return, both must sign)

Sign Here

It is unlawful to forge a spouse's/ RDP's signature.

Joint tax return? (See instructions.)

Your email address (optional). Enter only one email address. | Daytime phone number (optional) [redacted]

Paid preparer's signature (declaration of preparer is based on all information of which preparer has any knowledge): Lucina V. delosReyes 4/15/14

Firm's name (or yours, if self-employed): LUCINA V DE LOS REYES | • PTIN: P01204841

Firm's address: 1529 HAMPTON COURT NAPERVILLE, IL 60565 | • FEIN: 27-2432384

Do you want to allow another person to discuss this tax return with us? See instructions • [ ] Yes [X] No

Print Third Party Designee's Name | Telephone Number

TAXABLE YEAR **2013**

Wage and Tax Statement

CALIFORNIA SCHEDULE **W-2**

Important: Attach this form to the back of your Form 540, 540 2EZ, or Form 540NR (Long or Short).

Name(s) as shown on tax return: J[redacted]

SSN or ITIN: [redacted]

Caution: If this form is filled out do not send your Form(s) W-2 to the Franchise Tax Board. If your Form(s) W-2 are from multiple states, attach copies showing California tax withheld to this schedule. If this schedule is blank, attach your Form(s) W-2 to the lower front of your tax return.

All fields must be completed. DO NOT ATTACH PAYMENT TO THIS SCHEDULE.

* Employee's Social Security Number, name, and address must be the same as the information on the Form(s) W-2.

W-2 Information	1st W-2	2nd W-2
a. Employee's social security number *	[redacted]	[redacted]
b. Employer identification number (EIN)	[redacted]	[redacted]
c. Employer's name	IMPAQ REHABILITATION	HARDEN HOME HEALTH
Address	178 DENSLOWE DRIVE	3307 NORTHLAND STE 130
City	SAN FRANCISCO	AUSTIN
State	CA	TX
Zip Code	94132	78731
e. Employee's first, middle initial and last name*	[redacted]	[redacted]
f. Address*	[redacted]	[redacted]
City*	[redacted]	[redacted]
State*	[redacted]	[redacted]
Zip Code*	[redacted]	[redacted]
1. Wages, tips, other compensation	47,626.	455.
2. Federal income tax withheld	8,885.	36.
3. Social security wages	50,313.	455.
4. Social security tax withheld	3,119.	28.
6. Medicare tax withheld	730.	7.
7. Social security tips		
8. Allocated tips (not included in box 1)		
10. Dependent care benefits		
11. Nonqualified plans		

W-2 Information	1st W-2		2nd W-2	
12. Codes and amounts	Codes	Amounts	Codes	Amounts
	D	2,686.		
13. Check the appropriate box for: Statutory employee, Retirement plan, or Third-party sick pay	[ ] Statutory employee		[ ] Statutory employee	
	[X] Retirement plan		[ ] Retirement plan	
	[ ] Third-party sick pay		[ ] Third-party sick pay	
14. SDI, VPDI, or CA SDI (from box 14 or 19)	Type: CA SDI	Amount: 503.	Type: CA SDI	Amount: 5.
15. State and employer's State ID number	State: CA	Employer's state ID number: 262-0387 7	State: CA	Employer's state ID number: 010-6263-7
16. State wages, tips, etc.	47,626.		455.	
17. State income tax	3,169.			

TAXABLE YEAR

2013

Wage and Tax Statement

CALIFORNIA SCHEDULE

W-2

Important: Attach this form to the back of your Form 540, 540 2EZ, or Form 540NR (Long or Short).

Name(s) as shown on tax return | SSN or ITIN

Caution: If this form is filled out **do not** send your Form(s) W-2 to the Franchise Tax Board. If your Form(s) W-2 are from multiple states, **attach** copies showing California tax withheld to this schedule. If this schedule is blank, attach your Form(s) W-2 to the lower front of your tax return.

All fields must be completed. DO NOT ATTACH PAYMENT TO THIS SCHEDULE.

* Employee's Social Security Number, name, and address must be the same as the information on the Form(s) W-2.

W-2 Information	1st W-2	2nd W-2
a. Employee's social security number *		
b. Employer identification number (EIN)		
c. Employer's name	IMPAQ HEALTH SERVICES	
Address	2352 MARKET STREET	
City	SAN FRANCISCO	
State	CA	
Zip Code	94114	
e. Employee's first, middle initial and last name*		
f. Address*		
City*		
State*		
Zip Code*		
1. Wages, tips, other compensation	4,640.	
2. Federal income tax withheld	591.	
3. Social security wages	4,873.	
4. Social security tax withheld	302.	
6. Medicare tax withheld	71.	
7. Social security tips		
8. Allocated tips (not included in box 1)		
10. Dependent care benefits		
11. Nonqualified plans		

W-2 Information	1st W-2		2nd W-2	
12. Codes and amounts	Codes	Amounts	Codes	Amounts
	D	232.		
13. Check the appropriate box for: Statutory employee, Retirement plan, or Third-party sick pay	☐ Statutory employee		☐ Statutory employee	
	☐ Retirement plan		☐ Retirement plan	
	☐ Third-party sick pay		☐ Third-party sick pay	
14. SDI, VPDI, or CA SDI (from box 14 or 19)	Type: CA SDI	Amount: 49.	Type:	Amount:
15. State and employer's State ID number	State: CA	Employer's state ID number: 284-6364-4	State:	Employer's state ID number:
16. State wages, tips, etc.	4,640.			
17. State income tax	178.			

TAXABLE YEAR
2013

Additional Taxes on Qualified Plans (Including IRAs) and Other Tax-Favored Accounts

CALIFORNIA FORM
3805P

First name	Initial	Last name	SSN or ITIN
[redacted]		[redacted]	[redacted]
Address (number and street, PO Box, or PMB no.)		Apt. no./Ste. no.	Check this box if this is an amended return ☐
City		State	ZIP Code

Part I Additional Tax on Early Distributions - Complete this part if you received a taxable distribution, before you reached age 59 ½, from a qualified retirement plan (including an IRA) or modified endowment contract. You also may have to complete this part if you received a federal Form 1099-R that incorrectly indicates an early distribution or you received a Roth IRA distribution (see instructions).

1 Early distributions included in income. For Roth IRA distributions, see instructions . . . . 1 12,382.

2 Early distributions included on line 1 that are not subject to additional tax. See instructions. Enter the appropriate exception number from instructions ☐☐ 2

3 Amount subject to additional tax. Subtract line 2 from line 1* . . . . 3 12,382.

4 Tax due. Multiply line 3 by 2 ½ % (.025). Enter the amount here and include this amount in the total on Form 540, line 63 or Long Form 540NR, line 73. If you are not required to file a California income tax return, sign this form below and refer to the instructions 4 310.

* If any part of the amount on line 3 was a distribution from a SIMPLE IRA, you may have to include 6% (.06) of that amount on line 4 instead of 2 ½% (.025). See instructions.

Part II Additional Tax on Distributions from Coverdell Education Savings Accounts (ESAs) or Qualified Tuition Programs (QTPs) Not Used for Educational Expenses - Complete this part if a distribution was made from your Coverdell ESA or QTP and was not used for educational expenses.

5 Distributions included in income from Coverdell ESAs or QTPs. Enter the amount from federal Publication 970, Worksheet 7-3, line 16 5

6 Distributions included on line 5 that are not subject to additional tax. See instructions 6

7 Amount subject to additional tax. Subtract line 6 from line 5 7

8 Tax due. Multiply line 7 by 2 ½% (.025). Enter the amount here and include this amount in the total on Form 540, line 63 or Long Form 540NR, line 73. If you are not required to file a California income tax return, sign this form below and refer to the instructions 8 0.

Part III Additional Tax on Distributions from Archer and Medicare Advantage Medical Savings Accounts (MSAs) - Complete this part if you reported a taxable distribution from an MSA on federal Form 8853.

9 Taxable Archer MSA distribution from federal Form 8853, line 8 9

10 a If you meet any of the exceptions to the 10% tax (see instructions), check here . . . . 10a ☐

b Otherwise, multiply line 9 by 10% (.10). Enter the amount here and include this amount in the total on Form 540, line 63 or Long Form 540NR, line 73. If you are not required to file a California income tax return, sign this form below and refer to the instructions 10b

11 Additional tax due from Medicare Advantage MSA distributions. Enter the amount from federal Form 8853, line 13b. Also include this amount in the total on Form 540, line 63 or Long Form 540NR, line 73. If you are not required to file a California income tax return, sign this form below and refer to the instructions. Long Form 540NR filers, see instructions 11

Signature. Complete **only** if you are filing this form by itself and not with your tax return.

Under penalties of perjury, I declare that I have examined this return, including accompanying schedules and statements, and to the best of my knowledge and belief, it is true, correct, and complete. It is unlawful to forge a spouse's/registered domestic partner's signature.

Your signature
X

Date

Signature of paid preparer *(declaration of preparer is based on all information of which preparer has any knowledge.)*

PTIN

Firm's name (or yours if self-employed) and address

FEIN

TAXABLE YEAR **2013**

Underpayment of Estimated Tax by Individuals and Fiduciaries

CALIFORNIA FORM **5805**

Attach this form to **Side 2** of your Form 540, Long Form 540NR, or Form 541. Also, check the box for underpayment of estimated tax located on Form 540, line 113; Long Form 540NR, line 123; or Form 541, line 42, whichever applies.

Name(s) as shown on return: [redacted] SSN, ITIN or FEIN: [redacted]

IMPORTANT: In most cases, the Franchise Tax Board (FTB) can figure the penalty for you and you do not have to complete this form. See General Information B.

If you meet any of the following conditions, you do not owe a penalty for underpayment of estimated tax. **Do not complete or file this form if:**

- The amount of your tax liability (not including tax on lump-sum distributions) less credits (including the withholding credit) but not including estimated tax payments for either 2012 or 2013 was less than $500 (or less than $250 if married/RDP filing a separate return).
- Your 2012 return was for a full 12 months (or would have been if you were required to file) and you did not have any tax liability on that return.
- The amount of your withholding plus your estimated tax payments, **if paid in the required installments,** is at least 90% of the tax shown on your 2013 return or 100% of the tax shown on your 2012 return (110% if California adjusted gross income (AGI) was more than $150,000 or $75,000 if married/RDP filing a separate return) and you are not using the annualized income installment method. Taxpayers with California AGI equal to or greater than $1,000,000 (or $500,000 if married/RDP filing a separate return), must use the tax shown on their 2013 tax return if they do not meet one of the two conditions above.

Part I Questions. All filers must complete this part. Estates and Trusts, see General Information E.

1 Are you requesting a waiver of the penalty? If "Yes," provide an explanation below and be sure to check the box on Form 540, line 113; Long Form 540NR, line 123; or Form 541, line 42. If you need additional space, attach a statement. See General Information C . . . . . 1 ☐ Yes ☒ No

2 Did you use the annualized income installment method? If "Yes," see instructions for Part III and be sure to check the box on Form 540, line 113; Long Form 540NR, line 123; or Form 541, line 42. . . . . . 2 ☐ Yes ☒ No

3 Was your California withholding not withheld in equal installments and are you able to show the actual amounts withheld per period and the actual dates withheld? . . . . . 3 ☐ Yes ☒ No ☐ N/A

If "Yes," enter the **actual uneven amounts withheld** on the spaces provided below. The total of the four amounts must equal the total withholding reported on Form 540, line 71 and line 73; Form 540NR, line 81 and line 83; or Form 541, line 29 and line 31.

4/15/13 $________ ; 6/15/13 $________ ; 9/15/13 $________ ; 1/15/14 $________ .

4 For estates and trusts: Was the date of death less than two years from the end of the taxable year? See General Information E 4 ☐ Yes ☐ No

Part II Required Annual Payment. All filers must complete this part.

1	Current year tax. Enter your 2013 tax after credits. See instructions	1	5,427.
2	Multiply line 1 by 90% (.90)	2	4,884.
3	Withholding taxes. **Do not** include any estimated tax payments on this line. See instructions	3	3,347.
4	Subtract line 3 from line 1. If less than $500 (or less than $250 if married/RDP filing a separate return), stop here. You do not owe the penalty. **Do not** file form FTB 5805	4	2,080.
5	Enter the tax shown on your 2012 tax return. See instructions. (110% (1.10) of that amount if the adjusted gross income shown on that return is more than $150,000, or if married/RDP filing a separate return for 2013, more than $75,000).	5	8,583.
6	Required annual payment. Enter the **smaller** of line 2 or line 5. (If your California AGI is equal to or greater than $1,000,000/$500,000 for married/RDP filing a separate return, use line 2)	6	4,884.

Short Method

Caution: See the instructions to find out if you can use the short method. If you answered "Yes" to Question 2 in Part I, skip this part and go to Part III. If you answered "No" to Question 2 in Part I **and** you cannot use the short method, go to Worksheet II in the instructions.

7	Enter the amount, if any, from Part II, line 3 above	7	3,347.
8	Enter the total amount, if any, of estimated tax payments you made	8	
9	Add line 7 and line 8	9	3,347.
10	**Total underpayment for the year.** Subtract line 9 from line 6. If zero or less, stop here. You do not owe the penalty. **Do not** file form FTB 5805	10	1,537.
11	Multiply line 10 by .02121370	11	33.
12	• If the amount on line 10 was paid **on or after** 4/15/14, enter -0-. • If the amount on line 10 was paid **before** 4/15/14, enter the result of the following computation: Amount on line 10 X Number of days paid before 4/15/14 X .00008	12	
13	**PENALTY.** Subtract line 12 from line 11. Enter the result here and on Form 540, line 113; Long Form 540NR, line 123; or Form 541, line 42. Also, check the box for "FTB 5805." ▶	13	33.

Exhibit 8:

Copy of Bank Account Statements of Beneficiary's U.S. Citizen Brother

Bank of America

P.O. Box 15284
Wilmington, DE 19850

Customer service information

Customer service: 1.800.432.1000

TDD/TTY users only: 1.800.288.4408

En Español: 1.800.688.6086

bankofamerica.com

Bank of America, N.A.
P.O. Box 25118
Tampa, FL 33622-5118

Your combined statement

for September 08, 2016 to October 5, 2016

Your deposit accounts	Account/plan number	Ending balance	Details on
BofA Core Checking		$10,476.34	Page 3
Regular Savings		$8.63	Page 9
Total balance		**$10,484.97**	

IMPORTANT INFORMATION:
BANK DEPOSIT ACCOUNTS

Updating your contact information - We encourage you to keep your contact information up-to-date. This includes address, email and phone number. If your information has changed, the easiest way to update it is by visiting the Help & Support tab of Online Banking. Or, you can call our Customer Service team.

Deposit agreement - When you opened your account, you received a deposit agreement and fee schedule and agreed that your account would be governed by the terms of these documents, as we may amend them from time to time. These documents are part of the contract for your deposit account and govern all transactions relating to your account, including all deposits and withdrawals. Copies of both the deposit agreement and fee schedule which contain the current version of the terms and conditions of your account relationship may be obtained at our financial centers.

Electronic transfers: In case of errors or questions about your electronic transfers - If you think your statement or receipt is wrong or you need more information about an electronic transfer (e.g., ATM transactions, direct deposits or withdrawals, point-of-sale transactions) on the statement or receipt, telephone or write us at the address and number listed on the front of this statement as soon as you can. We must hear from you no later than 60 days after we sent you the FIRST statement on which the error or problem appeared.

- Tell us your name and account number.
- Describe the error or transfer you are unsure about, and explain as clearly as you can why you believe there is an error or why you need more information.
- Tell us the dollar amount of the suspected error.

For consumer accounts used primarily for personal, family or household purposes, we will investigate your complaint and will correct any error promptly. If we take more than 10 business days (10 calendar days if you are a Massachusetts customer) (20 business days if you are a new customer, for electronic transfers occurring during the first 30 days after the first deposit is made to your account) to do this, we will credit your account for the amount you think is in error, so that you will have use of the money during the time it will take to complete our investigation.

For other accounts, we investigate, and if we find we have made an error, we credit your account at the conclusion of our investigation.

Reporting other problems - You must examine your statement carefully and promptly. You are in the best position to discover errors and unauthorized transactions on your account. If you fail to notify us in writing of suspected problems or an unauthorized transaction within the time period specified in the deposit agreement (which periods are no more than 60 days after we make the statement available to you and in some cases are 30 days or less), we are not liable to you for, and you agree to not make a claim against us for the problems or unauthorized transactions.

Direct deposits - If you have arranged to have direct deposits made to your account at least once every 60 days from the same person or company, you may call us at the telephone number listed on the front of this statement to find out if the deposit was made as scheduled. You may also review your activity online or visit a financial center for information.

Bank of America

Your checking account

Your BofA Core Checking

Account summary

Beginning balance on September 8, 2016	$155.18
Deposits and other additions	29,665.22
ATM and debit card subtractions	-8,596.02
Other subtractions	-9,863.04
Checks	-695.00
Service fees	-190.00
Ending balance on October 5, 2016	**$10,476.34**

Deposits and other additions

Date	Description	Amount
09/08/16	Online Banking transfer from SAV 5143 Confirmation# 0530506922	30.21
09/09/16	AMITY HOME HEALT DES:DIRECT DEP ID:285066425113SXR INDN:CAPISTRANO,JOSE CO ID:9111111101 PPD	3,250.00
09/09/16	BKOFAMERICA ATM 09/09 #000001285 DEPOSIT A P GIANNINI SAN MATEO CA	1,408.00
09/12/16	BKOFAMERICA ATM 09/12 #000004175 DEPOSIT A P GIANNINI SAN MATEO CA	1,800.00
09/14/16	OVERDRAFT PROTECTION FROM 4264287983276615	88.01
09/14/16	BKOFAMERICA ATM 09/14 #000001569 DEPOSIT 21ST AND IRVING SAN FRANCISCO CA	100.00
09/15/16	BKOFAMERICA ATM 09/15 #000004977 DEPOSIT A P GIANNINI SAN MATEO CA	500.00
09/19/16	BKOFAMERICA ATM 09/19 #000007340 DEPOSIT A P GIANNINI SAN MATEO CA	205.00
09/20/16	Overdraft Fee Credit	5.00

continued on the next page

Deposits and other additions - continued

Date	Description	Amount
09/23/16	AMITY HOME HEALT DES:DIRECT DEP ID:699068213200SXR INDN:CAPISTRANO,JOSE CO ID:9111111101 PPD	3,715.00
09/26/16	BKOFAMERICA ATM 09/25 #000001798 DEPOSIT A P GIANNINI SAN MATEO CA	100.00
09/27/16	OVERDRAFT PROTECTION FROM 4264287983276615	100.00
09/27/16	BKOFAMERICA ATM 09/27 #000002546 DEPOSIT A P GIANNINI SAN MATEO CA	3,920.00
10/03/16	Counter Credit	2,176.00
10/03/16	Online Banking transfer from SAV 5143 Confirmation# 3233849100	80.00
10/05/16	BKOFAMERICA ATM 10/05 #000007672 DEPOSIT A P GIANNINI SAN MATEO CA	10,000.00
10/05/16	Counter Credit	2,188.00
Total deposits and other additions		**$29,665.22**

Withdrawals and other subtractions

ATM and debit card subtractions

Date	Description	Amount
09/09/16	CHECKCARD 0908 HUMMUS MED SAN MATEO CA 24055236253286926301634	-24.03
09/09/16	CHECKCARD 0908 HUMMUS MED SAN MATEO CA 24055236253286926301758	-10.74
09/09/16	CHECKCARD 0908 SQ *CHATIME SAN MATEO CA 24492156252740324546507	-5.00
09/09/16	7-ELEVEN 09/09 #000147253 PURCHASE 7-ELEVEN SAN MATEO CA	-19.63
09/09/16	BKOFAMERICA ATM 09/09 #000001286 WITHDRWL A P GIANNINI SAN MATEO CA	-600.00
09/12/16	CHECKCARD 0909 FACEBK *2LRTFANLS2 fb.me/cc CA 24692166253000324280557	-99.99
09/12/16	CHECKCARD 0909 FACEBK *A38EDA2MS2 fb.me/cc CA 24692166253000499028443	-99.99
09/12/16	CHECKCARD 0909 FACEBK *YSSBEAELS2 fb.me/cc CA 24692166253000499057483	-49.99
09/12/16	CHECKCARD 0909 MERCURY*INSURANCE 888-637-2176 CA 24692166253000609582248	-226.22
09/12/16	CHECKCARD 0909 ZEN NOODLE SAN MATEO CA 24755426254152541600777	-23.35
09/12/16	CHECKCARD 0909 SQ *CHATIME SAN MATEO CA 24492156253740330672296	-8.27
09/12/16	CHECKCARD 0909 CHECK N GO COLLECTIONS 513-2296745 OH 24717056254132542553045	-200.00
09/12/16	CHECKCARD 0909 LOAN BY PHONE CALIFORNI 877-5777977 TN 24383446254006784546063	-300.00
09/12/16	CHECKCARD 0910 TIV*TIVO SERVICE 877-367-8486 CA 24692166254000884629937	-12.99
09/12/16	CHECKCARD 0910 UBER US SEP09 Q4MT3 HELP.UBER.COMCA 24492156254719594717749	-38.23
09/12/16	CHECKCARD 0910 GOOGLE *Zynga Inc g.co/payhelp#CA 24692166254000133790852	-29.99
09/12/16	CHECKCARD 0910 UBER US SEP09 QS6EZ HELP.UBER.COMCA 24492156254719606209081	-38.43
09/12/16	CHECKCARD 0910 FACEBK *M79Y3BWLS2 fb.me/cc CA 24692166254000141509252	-29.99
09/12/16	CHECKCARD 0910 MIMIS CAFE 32 FOSTER CITY CA 24445006255100265587667	-31.50
09/12/16	CHECKCARD 0910 AT&T*BILL PAYMENT WWW.ATT.COM TX 24493986254799458348566 RECURRING	-198.20

continued on the next page

Withdrawals and other subtractions - continued

ATM and debit card subtractions - continued

Date	Description	Amount
09/12/16	7-ELEVEN 09/10 #000031276 PURCHASE 7-ELEVEN SOUTH SAN FRA CA	-17.97
09/12/16	CHECKCARD 0911 UBER TECHNOLOGIES INC 866-576-1039 CA 24692166255000436422137	-42.13
09/12/16	CHECKCARD 0911 UBER US SEP10 K53VI HELP.UBER.COMCA 24492156255719636159255	-7.78
09/12/16	ELEMENTS PETRO 09/11 #000219808 PURCHASE ELEMENTS PETROL BERKELEY CA	-9.30
09/12/16	CHECKCARD 0911 UBER US SEP11 TQIPQ HELP.UBER.COMCA 24492156255719641219219	-37.02
09/12/16	CHECKCARD 0911 ZEN NOODLE SAN MATEO CA 24755426256132566084543	-21.62
09/12/16	SAN MATEO VALE 09/12 #000871640 PURCHASE SAN MATEO VALERO SAN MATEO CA	-8.09
09/12/16	BKOFAMERICA ATM 09/12 #000002868 WITHDRWL WARM SPRINGS FREMONT CA	-40.00
09/13/16	CHECKCARD 0911 FACEBK *NZ57JASLS2 fb.me/cc CA 24692166256000248601398	-99.99
09/13/16	CHECKCARD 0912 GOOGLE *Zynga Inc g.co/payhelp#CA 24692166256000066228118	-29.99
09/13/16	CHECKCARD 0912 FACEBK *QXLPKAJLS2 fb.me/cc CA 24692166256000148671228	-99.99
09/13/16	CHECKCARD 0912 FIVE GUYS #CA-1563 BELMONT CA 24224436257101009665839	-13.71
09/13/16	CHECKCARD 0913 COMCAST CALIFORNIA 800-COMCAST CA 24692166257000440579292 RECURRING	-209.50
09/14/16	CHECKCARD 0914 FACEBK *R5KUFANLS2 fb.me/cc CA 24692166258000909897499	-1.99
09/14/16	CHECKCARD 0912 SAN MATEO VALERO SAN MATEO CA 24427336257120005659320	-47.30
09/14/16	CHECKCARD 0913 MCC HOMEOWNERS GW 888-637-2176 CA 24692166257000543247920	-131.00
09/14/16	CHECKCARD 0913 FACEBK *XZ88JASLS2 fb.me/cc CA 24692166257000713519587	-49.99
09/14/16	CHECKCARD 0913 FACEBK *7298JASLS2 fb.me/cc CA 24692166257000713518639	-99.99
09/14/16	CHECKCARD 0913 FACEBK *P298JASLS2 fb.me/cc CA 24692166257000713521674	-99.99
09/15/16	CHECKCARD 0913 STARBUCKS STORE 05844 SAN MATEO CA 24692166258000286519286	-4.93
09/15/16	CHECKCARD 0915 UBER US SEP14 CYL4P HELP.UBER.COMCA 24492156259719720698545	-38.14
09/16/16	CHECKCARD 0915 UBER US SEP14 YGPY5 HELP.UBER.COMCA 24492156259719727912923	-42.02
09/19/16	CHECKCARD 0915 WHISPERS CAFE & CREPER BELMONT CA 24269796260500804301631	-18.53
09/19/16	CHECKCARD 0918 FEDEX 784112975148 MEMPHIS TN 24164076262741210928325	-26.75
09/19/16	CHECKCARD 0917 FEDEXOFFICE 00003491 SAN MATEO CA 24164076262069192995793	-4.26
09/19/16	CHECKCARD 0918 UBER US SEP17 WSGEY HELP.UBER.COMCA 24492156262719800618038	-40.02
09/23/16	BKOFAMERICA ATM 09/23 #000002272 WITHDRWL COLUMBUS SAN FRANCISCO CA	-520.00
09/23/16	BKOFAMERICA ATM 09/23 #000001586 WITHDRWL COLUMBUS SAN FRANCISCO CA	-100.00
09/26/16	CHECKCARD 0923 JACK IN THE BOX 495 SAN MATEO CA 24435656268091929001386	-14.38
09/26/16	CHECKCARD 0925 LITTLE CAESARS 1671 000 SAN MATEO CA 24445006270000619885802	-12.01

continued on the next page

Withdrawals and other subtractions - continued

ATM and debit card subtractions - continued

Date	Description	Amount
09/26/16	CHECKCARD 0925 LITTLE CAESARS 1671 000 SAN MATEO CA 24445006270000619885984	-7.19
09/26/16	7-ELEVEN 09/25 #000508816 PURCHASE 7-ELEVEN SAN MATEO CA	-7.35
09/28/16	CHECKCARD 0927 SQ *CHATIME SAN MATEO CA 24492156271740324581808	-5.00
09/28/16	CHECKCARD 0927 HUMMUS MED SAN MATEO CA 24055236272286926301987	-27.31
09/29/16	CHECKCARD 0928 REMITLY 877-526-4216 WA 24493986273026905077268	-2,279.62
09/30/16	CHECKCARD 0928 SHANG KEE BAKERY SAN MATEO CA 24275506273448400464918	-20.26
09/30/16	CHECKCARD 0928 TOTAL ACCOUNT RECOVERY LENEXA KS 24473016273900016651528	-757.50
09/30/16	CHECKCARD 0928 SAN MATEO VALERO SAN MATEO CA 24427336273120005802557	-30.62
09/30/16	CHECKCARD 0929 JAMBA JUICE-#69 REDWOOD CITY CA 24431066274286388900833	-10.46
09/30/16	7-ELEVEN 09/29 #000600439 PURCHASE 7-ELEVEN SAN MATEO CA	-37.71
10/03/16	CHECKCARD 0928 KAISER CPP PHARM 256 LIVERMORE CA 24431066274869000816303	-100.00
10/03/16	CHECKCARD 0929 KAISER CPP PHARM 256 LIVERMORE CA 24431066274869000750320	-297.12
10/03/16	CHECKCARD 0929 KAISER CPP PHARM 256 LIVERMORE CA 24431066274869000760006	-50.00
10/03/16	CHECKCARD 0929 KAISER CPP PHARM 256 LIVERMORE CA 24431066274869000734092	-125.00
10/03/16	CHECKCARD 0929 ZEN NOODLE SAN MATEO CA 24755426274162749018033	-20.75
10/03/16	CHECKCARD 1001 SAN MATEO VALERO SAN MATEO CA 24427336276120005871351	-24.22
10/03/16	SAN MATEO VALE 10/01 #000494583 PURCHASE SAN MATEO VALERO SAN MATEO CA	-1.00
10/03/16	CHECKCARD 1001 NEPENJI JAPAN CENTER BE SAN FRANCISCOCA 24055236276200365800678	-60.00
10/05/16	CHECKCARD 1004 FACEBK *RCDQMAELS2 fb.me/cc CA 24692166278000797320097	-99.99
10/05/16	CHECKCARD 1004 FACEBK *PCDQMAELS2 fb.me/cc CA 24692166278000797320022	-99.99
10/05/16	CHECKCARD 1004 WELL THERAPY GROUP 415-952-0290 CA 24707806278980167721327	-600.00
Total ATM and debit card subtractions		**-$8,596.02**

Other subtractions

Date	Description	Amount
09/09/16	KEEP THE CHANGE TRANSFER TO ACCT 5143 FOR 09/09/16	-1.60
09/12/16	KEEP THE CHANGE TRANSFER TO ACCT 5143 FOR 09/12/16	-8.95
09/13/16	Metropolitan DES:CHECK PMTS CHECK #:0891 INDN:Jose Capistrano CO ID:1752788861 ARC	-2,869.70
09/13/16	AMERICAN EXPRESS DES:ACH PMT ID:V3086 INDN:JOSE CAPISTRANO CO ID:1133133497 PPD	-110.00
09/13/16	KEEP THE CHANGE TRANSFER CANCELED-LOW ACCT BALANCE	0.00
09/14/16	KEEP THE CHANGE TRANSFER TO ACCT 5143 FOR 09/14/16	-0.74
09/15/16	KEEP THE CHANGE TRANSFER TO ACCT 5143 FOR 09/15/16	-0.93

continued on the next page

Withdrawals and other subtractions - continued

Other subtractions - continued

Date	Description	Amount
09/16/16	TARGET FINANCE DES:1111111111 ID:2262303 INDN:JOSE CAPISTRANO CO ID:9004240778 PPD PMT INFO:TARGET FINANCE	-402.67
09/16/16	KEEP THE CHANGE TRANSFER TO ACCT 5143 FOR 09/16/16	-0.98
09/19/16	DISCOVER DES:E-PAYMENT ID:3345 INDN:CAPISTRANO JOSE CO ID:3510020270 PPD	-195.00
09/19/16	GARDEN STATE DES:GARDEN ST ID:0905534332 INDN:JOSE P CAPISTRA0801001 CO ID:6221700753 PPD	-30.00
09/19/16	KEEP THE CHANGE TRANSFER CANCELED-LOW ACCT BALANCE	-0.00
09/20/16	CAPITAL ONE DES:CRCARDPMT ID:626330189065158 INDN:8887273572CAPISTRANOJO CO ID:9541719018 TEL	-87.00
09/21/16	COMENITYCARD PAY DES:CHECK PYMT CHECK #:760 INDN:0000000344688838 0077 CO ID:9311429215 ARC	-50.00
09/22/16	CHASE CREDIT CARDS Bill Payment	-63.00
09/23/16	Online Banking transfer to SAV 5143 Confirmation# 2261659984	-80.00
09/23/16	Online Banking payment to CRD 6615 Confirmation# 1861806605	-385.00
09/23/16	TARGET CASH NOW DES:8773349416 ID:160922OC23951NW INDN:JOSE CAPISTRANO CO ID:1800872072 WEB	-1,656.37
09/23/16	VBS Arrow One DES:8558363647 ID:4480089266 INDN:JOSE CAPISTRANO CO ID:18026849 PPD	-214.50
09/23/16	Online scheduled payment to CRD 0490 Confirmation# 1262958802	-200.00
09/23/16	CHASE CARD SERVICES Bill Payment	-107.00
09/26/16	CLUB LOSGATO ABC DES:CLUB FEES ID:1626700470765 INDN:JOSE CAPISTRANO CO ID:1710602737 PPD PMT INFO: - THE CLUB LOS GATOS 888-827-9262	-120.00
09/26/16	KEEP THE CHANGE TRANSFER CANCELED-LOW ACCT BALANCE	-0.00
09/28/16	KEEP THE CHANGE TRANSFER TO ACCT 5143 FOR 09/28/16	-0.69
09/29/16	KEEP THE CHANGE TRANSFER TO ACCT 5143 FOR 09/29/16	-0.38
09/30/16	KEEP THE CHANGE TRANSFER TO ACCT 5143 FOR 09/30/16	-2.45
10/03/16	Online Banking transfer to SAV 5143 Confirmation# 2530378149	-80.00
10/03/16	SPNG FIN PPD PAY DES:LOAN P-PAY ID:121607397369 INDN:CAPISTRANO,,JOSEP, CO ID:1350416090 PPD	-818.15
10/03/16	KEEP THE CHANGE TRANSFER TO ACCT 5143 FOR 10/03/16	-1.91
10/04/16	RETURN ITEM CHARGEBACK	-2,176.00
10/05/16	Online scheduled payment to CRD 0490 Confirmation# 4371202284	-200.00
10/05/16	KEEP THE CHANGE TRANSFER TO ACCT 5143 FOR 10/05/16	-0.02
Total other subtractions		**-$9,863.04**

Bank of America

P.O. Box 15284
Wilmington, DE 19850

Customer service information

Customer service: 1.800.432.1000

TDD/TTY users only: 1.800.288.4408

En Español: 1.800.688.6086

bankofamerica.com

Bank of America, N.A.
P.O. Box 25118
Tampa, FL 33622-5118

Your combined statement

for October 06, 2016 to November 3, 2016

Your deposit accounts	Account/plan number	Ending balance	Details on
BofA Core Checking		$527.92	Page 3
Regular Savings		-$4.06	Page 7
Total balance		**$523.86**	

IMPORTANT INFORMATION:
BANK DEPOSIT ACCOUNTS

Updating your contact information - We encourage you to keep your contact information up-to-date. This includes address, email and phone number. If your information has changed, the easiest way to update it is by visiting the Help & Support tab of Online Banking. Or, you can call our Customer Service team.

Deposit agreement - When you opened your account, you received a deposit agreement and fee schedule and agreed that your account would be governed by the terms of these documents, as we may amend them from time to time. These documents are part of the contract for your deposit account and govern all transactions relating to your account, including all deposits and withdrawals. Copies of both the deposit agreement and fee schedule which contain the current version of the terms and conditions of your account relationship may be obtained at our financial centers.

Electronic transfers: In case of errors or questions about your electronic transfers - If you think your statement or receipt is wrong or you need more information about an electronic transfer (e.g., ATM transactions, direct deposits or withdrawals, point-of-sale transactions) on the statement or receipt, telephone or write us at the address and number listed on the front of this statement as soon as you can. We must hear from you no later than 60 days after we sent you the FIRST statement on which the error or problem appeared.

- Tell us your name and account number.
- Describe the error or transfer you are unsure about, and explain as clearly as you can why you believe there is an error or why you need more information.
- Tell us the dollar amount of the suspected error.

For consumer accounts used primarily for personal, family or household purposes, we will investigate your complaint and will correct any error promptly. If we take more than 10 business days (10 calendar days if you are a Massachusetts customer) (20 business days if you are a new customer, for electronic transfers occurring during the first 30 days after the first deposit is made to your account) to do this, we will credit your account for the amount you think is in error, so that you will have use of the money during the time it will take to complete our investigation.

For other accounts, we investigate, and if we find we have made an error, we credit your account at the conclusion of our investigation.

Reporting other problems - You must examine your statement carefully and promptly. You are in the best position to discover errors and unauthorized transactions on your account. If you fail to notify us in writing of suspected problems or an unauthorized transaction within the time period specified in the deposit agreement (which periods are no more than 60 days after we make the statement available to you and in some cases are 30 days or less), we are not liable to you for, and you agree to not make a claim against us for the problems or unauthorized transactions.

Direct deposits - If you have arranged to have direct deposits made to your account at least once every 60 days from the same person or company, you may call us at the telephone number listed on the front of this statement to find out if the deposit was made as scheduled. You may also review your activity online or visit a financial center for information.

Bank of America

Your checking account

Your BofA Core Checking

Account summary

Beginning balance on October 6, 2016	$10,476.34
Deposits and other additions	11,200.00
ATM and debit card subtractions	-5,144.71
Other subtractions	-13,641.44
Checks	-2,359.27
Service fees	-3.00
Ending balance on November 3, 2016	**$527.92**

Deposits and other additions

Date	Description		Amount
10/07/16	AMITY HOME HEALT DES:DIRECT DEP ID:937901045884SXR INDN:CAPISTRANO,JOSE ID:9111111101 PPD	CO	4,785.00
10/21/16	AMITY HOME HEALT DES:DIRECT DEP ID:310028178985SXR INDN:CAPISTRANO,JOSE ID:9111111101 PPD	CO	5,342.00
10/25/16	Online Banking transfer from SAV 5143 Confirmation# 2541212417		29.00
10/25/16	Online Banking transfer from SAV 5143 Confirmation# 2441209058		20.00
11/02/16	Counter Credit		1,024.00
Total deposits and other additions			**$11,200.00**

Withdrawals and other subtractions

ATM and debit card subtractions

Date	Description	Amount
10/06/16	CHEVRON/JOHN C 10/06 #000562023 PURCHASE CHEVRON/JOHN CONW MENLO PARK CA	-6.28
10/07/16	CHECKCARD 0930 KAISER CPP PHARM 256 LIVERMORE CA 24431066280869000776574	-124.75
10/07/16	CHECKCARD 1005 LITTLE CAESARS 1671 000 SAN MATEO CA 24445006280500521816041	-19.18
10/07/16	CHECKCARD 1006 REMITLY 877-526-4216 WA 24493986281026939100409	-429.70
10/07/16	CHECKCARD 1006 CHEVRON 0204447 MENLO PARK CA 24692166280000125972482	-54.93
10/07/16	BKOFAMERICA ATM 10/07 #000007511 WITHDRWL MISSION PLAZA SAN FRANCISCO CA	-600.00
10/11/16	CHECKCARD 1007 FEDEXOFFICE 00003491 SAN MATEO CA 24164076281069229428161	-1.89
10/11/16	CHECKCARD 1008 1028 SPENGERS BERKELEY SAN FRANCISCOCA 24431066283286488900351	-261.70
10/11/16	CHECKCARD 1008 GOOGLE *Zynga Inc g.co/payhelp#CA 24692166282000232272394	-99.99
10/11/16	CHECKCARD 1008 MANILA EATERY COLMA CA 24224436283103001613609	-40.60
10/11/16	7-ELEVEN 10/09 #000861813 PURCHASE 7-ELEVEN SAN MATEO CA	-34.37
10/11/16	WHOLEFDS CAS # 10/11 #000602046 PURCHASE WHOLEFDS CAS #10 SAN FRANCISCO CA	-44.21
10/11/16	SHELL Service 10/11 #000397781 PURCHASE SHELL Service Sta SOUTH SAN FRA CA	-64.77
10/11/16	SHELL Service 10/11 #000715287 PURCHASE SHELL Service Sta SOUTH SAN FRA CA	-13.32
10/11/16	7-ELEVEN 10/11 #000814549 PURCHASE 7-ELEVEN SAN MATEO CA	-11.24
10/12/16	CHECKCARD 1011 REMITLY 877-526-4216 WA 24493986286026954416842	-428.35
10/12/16	CHECKCARD 1011 FEDEXOFFICE 00003491 SAN MATEO CA 24164076285069234764366	-6.57
10/12/16	7-ELEVEN 10/12 #000920325 PURCHASE 7-ELEVEN SAN MATEO CA	-7.53
10/13/16	CHECKCARD 1011 STARBUCKS STORE 00613 SAN MATEO CA 24692166286000430758174	-18.70
10/13/16	CHECKCARD 1012 ZEN NOODLE SAN MATEO CA 24755426287732878267935	-19.11
10/14/16	7-ELEVEN 10/14 #000414419 PURCHASE 7-ELEVEN SAN MATEO CA	-13.70
10/17/16	CHECKCARD 1014 MAMA MIA PIZZA BRISBANE CA 24801636288200299000092	-54.74
10/17/16	CHECKCARD 1015 1028 SPENGERS BERKELEY SAN FRANCISCOCA 24431066290286488900154	-110.05
10/17/16	BKOFAMERICA ATM 10/14 #000004677 WITHDRWL A P GIANNINI SAN MATEO CA	-700.00
10/17/16	DRAEGER'S SAN 10/14 #000473168 PURCHASE DRAEGER'S SAN MAT SAN MATEO CA	-125.34
10/17/16	CHECKCARD 1015 CHEVRON 0097927 HALF MOON BAYCA 24692166290000430641119	-49.97
10/17/16	SHELL Service 10/15 #000904632 PURCHASE SHELL Service Sta HALF MOON BAY CA	-6.50
10/17/16	7-ELEVEN 10/16 #000665724 PURCHASE 7-ELEVEN SAN MATEO CA	-7.20
10/17/16	7-ELEVEN 10/17 #000009340 PURCHASE 7-ELEVEN SAN MATEO CA	-8.32
10/18/16	CHECKCARD 1017 THE BAY FISH AND CHIPS SUNNYVALE CA 24431066292200295400132	-27.36
10/18/16	7-ELEVEN 10/18 #000455001 PURCHASE 7-ELEVEN SAN MATEO CA	-19.39
10/19/16	BKOFAMERICA ATM 10/18 #000005238 WITHDRWL A P GIANNINI SAN MATEO CA	-700.00
10/24/16	CHECKCARD 1021 REMITLY 877-526-4216 WA 24493986296026769487366	-698.43

continued on the next page

Withdrawals and other subtractions - continued

ATM and debit card subtractions - continued

Date	Description	Amount
10/24/16	BKOFAMERICA ATM 10/22 #000008965 WITHDRWL A P GIANNINI SAN MATEO CA	-200.00
10/24/16	CHECKCARD 1022 1028 SPENGERS BERKELEY SAN FRANCISCOCA 24431066297286488900025	-126.02
10/25/16	CHECKCARD 1023 TORPEDO ROOM BERKELEY CA 24493986298207199700424	-10.50
Total ATM and debit card subtractions		**-$5,144.71**

Other subtractions

Date	Description	Amount
10/06/16	Bank of America Credit Card Bill Payment	-500.00
10/06/16	KEEP THE CHANGE TRANSFER TO ACCT 5143 FOR 10/06/16	-0.72
10/07/16	Automatic Transfer to CHK 5143 Confirmation# 1083396274	-25.00
10/07/16	KEEP THE CHANGE TRANSFER TO ACCT 5143 FOR 10/07/16	-1.44
10/11/16	KEEP THE CHANGE TRANSFER TO ACCT 5143 FOR 10/11/16	-3.91
10/12/16	CA TLR cash withdrawal from CHK 4909	-7,000.00
10/12/16	KEEP THE CHANGE TRANSFER TO ACCT 5143 FOR 10/12/16	-1.55
10/13/16	KEEP THE CHANGE TRANSFER TO ACCT 5143 FOR 10/13/16	-1.19
10/14/16	KEEP THE CHANGE TRANSFER TO ACCT 5143 FOR 10/14/16	-0.30
10/17/16	KEEP THE CHANGE TRANSFER TO ACCT 5143 FOR 10/17/16	-3.88
10/18/16	KEEP THE CHANGE TRANSFER TO ACCT 5143 FOR 10/18/16	-1.25
10/19/16	Online scheduled payment to CRD 0490 Confirmation# 1987519067	-200.00
10/19/16	DISCOVER DES:E-PAYMENT ID:3345 INDN:CAPISTRANO JOSE CO ID:3510020270 PPD	-174.00
10/19/16	GARDEN STATE DES:GARDEN ST ID:0905534332 INDN:JOSE P CAPISTRA0801001 CO ID:6221700753 PPD	-30.00
10/20/16	CAPITAL ONE DES:CRCARDPMT ID:629330189006573 INDN:8887273572CAPISTRANOJO CO ID:9541719018 TEL	-88.00
10/21/16	CHASE CARD SERVICES Bill Payment	-107.00
10/21/16	CHASE CREDIT CARDS Bill Payment	-63.00
10/24/16	SPNG FIN PPD PAY DES:LOAN P-PAY ID:121607397369 INDN:CAPISTRANO,,JOSEP, CO ID:1350416090 PPD	-818.15
10/24/16	KEEP THE CHANGE TRANSFER TO ACCT 5143 FOR 10/24/16	-1.55
10/25/16	CA TLR cash withdrawal from CHK 4909	-4,000.00
10/25/16	CLUB LOSGATO ABC DES:CLUB FEES ID:1629800156866 INDN:JOSE CAPISTRANO CO ID:1710602737 PPD PMT INFO: - THE CLUB LOS GATOS 888-827-9262	-120.00

continued on the next page

Withdrawals and other subtractions - continued

Other subtractions - continued

Date	Description	Amount
10/25/16	KEEP THE CHANGE TRANSFER TO ACCT 5143 FOR 10/25/16	-0.50
11/03/16	CA TLR cash withdrawal from CHK 4909	-300.00
11/03/16	Online scheduled payment to CRD 0490 Confirmation# 3117144718	-200.00
Total other subtractions		**-$13,641.44**

Checks

Date	Check #	Amount	Date	Check #	Amount
10/20/16	753	-30.00	10/11/16	5485*	-184.66
10/24/16	981*	-90.00	10/24/16	5719*	-84.61
10/20/16	1012*	-1,500.00	10/17/16	6512*	-20.00
10/11/16	1089*	-150.00	10/11/16	6617*	-300.00
			Total checks		**-$2,359.27**
			Total # of checks		**8**

* *There is a gap in sequential check numbers*

Service fees

Your Overdraft and NSF: Returned Item fees for this statement period and year to date are shown below.

	Total for this period	Total year-to-date
Total Overdraft fees	$0.00	$1,435.00
Total NSF: Returned Item fees	$0.00	$910.00

We refunded to you a total of $385.00 in fees for Overdraft and/or NSF: Returned Items this year.

Attention: You have 20 or more overdraft and returned item fees on your account this year.

We are here to help – talk with us about ways you can help avoid fees, keep better track of your account activity, and make sure you have the account that is right for you.

Please call the number on this statement, or go to bankofamerica.com/appointments to schedule an appointment with us at a time that works for you.

Date	Transaction description	Amount
11/03/16	Check Image Service Fee	-3.00
Total service fees		**-$3.00**

Note your Ending Balance already reflects the subtraction of Service Fees.

www.ingramcontent.com/pod-product-compliance
Lightning Source LLC
Chambersburg PA
CBHW061356240926
51846CB00007B/1423
9781948774871